Social Studies in the Storytelling Classroom

"For children, we know that the structure of stories is a powerful link to comprehension. I would say that in working with adults in teacher education I have learned that a good story is worth a thousand pages of reading. They remember the story as a mnemonic for the principle."

DR. CAMILLE BLACHOWICZ, *PH.D., Distinguished Research Professor, National College of Education, National Louis University*

"A delightfully diverse and thoroughly practical set of curriculum-based storytelling units, providing an inexhaustible resource for educational storytellers and classroom teachers."

JOSEPH SOBOL, PH.D., *professor of Curriculum and Instruction, East Tennessee State University*

"These roadmaps will guide our children and grandchildren to remember the stories we told and to reflect on when, where and why we told them. We need this kind of reflection and scholarship. All too often, we forget to honor the origin."

EMILY HOOPER LANSANA, *Community Partnerships Manager for the Arts and Public Life Initiative and the Reva and David Logan Center for the Arts, University of Chicago*

"In order to construct a classroom community of accepting and respectful learners, children must first have the aptitude to understand themselves and their representation in the classroom and the world around them. This book does a courageous job at facilitating an understanding of the essentials needed for ensuring that children make the connections through stories and storytelling. **This is a "must have" on every teacher's bookshelf!"**

TRACY DRUMMER-AIDEN, *Kindergarten Teacher, Baker Demonstration School, Evanston, Illinois*

"Each chapter is thoughtful, original and seems to touch on the current direction of educating students to be critical thinkers. This is a really, really good book."

DIANE WILLIAMS, *co-author, co-editor with Stenson and Norfolk of Literacy Development in the Storytelling Classroom and The Storytelling Classroom:Applications across the Curriculum*

"The writing team of Sherry Norfolk and Jane Stenson has done it again. What they have achieved in previous publications for literacy development and cross-curricular applications of storytelling, they now have accomplished with storytelling and the teaching of history, culture, geography, and identity. Written in accordance with national standards, and with clearly-articulated, teacher-friendly units and objectives, this book will be indispensable for those who wish to enliven their classrooms with empathy and creativity. Norfolk and Stenson have found a way to put "story" back in "hi***story***;" calling upon many of the nation's most charismatic storytellers to contribute to their work. **History is more than facts and dates; in this text worlds come vividly to life when animated by stories.** If Daniel Pink, the author of A Whole New Mind is correct in his assertion that story and empathy will be essential skills for the 21st century, then this dynamic text will assume ever increasing prominence as it empowers teachers to make a difference. Lucid, inspiring, and pedagogically sound, this work makes a compelling argument that what we need more than "smart" classrooms are classrooms that are "wise." The foremost authorities writing about the intersection of storytelling and education in the country, Norfolk and Stenson have added an extraordinary new work to the canon."

RIVES COLLINS, *immediate Past President, American Alliance for Theatre and Education; Associate Professor, Northwestern University*

"As social studies teachers, we've known for generations about the power of stories to connect students to history, to each other and to people around the globe. The tellers and teachers who contributed to this enlightening volume provide stories, lessons and tools to help our students become and stay connected. Read it and connect yourself to a worthy tradition."

RICH KATZ, *middle school social studies teacher, Evanston, IL*

"With clarity and precision these noted storytellers and educators share their experience and expertise, enabling teachers to bring history to life in the classroom and give voice to the forgotten faces and stories of the past."

KAREN CHACE, *New England storyteller and teaching artist*

"Gifted educators and storytellers from across the United States offer accessible but inspirational ways to make storytelling a portal to faceted insights about culture, history, geography, and identity. This handbook, organized around the National Council for the Social Studies standards, offers lesson and program ideas adaptable to any classroom or library setting.

JANICE M. DEL NEGRO, PH.D., *GSLIS Dominican University*

"What a rich resource for educators — filled with innovative classroom activities to engage and challenge learners. The 'art' of teaching for memorable learning is back!"

SUE BLACK, *Storyteller / Teaching Artist / Certified Bullying Prevention Trainer*

"I couldn't put this book down, the stories were so riveting! You'll never teach about the Civil War, Native Americans, or the Holocaust the same way again once you've lived through these experiences with the historical, multi-cultural characters in this book. Who knew that you could learn so much about geography, history, and our own identities from those tricksters, coyote and fox—and from what Native Americans buy at Walmart? This collection proves once and for all that we can teach to the national standards through imaginative, exciting lessons that develop our full humanity. A must for anyone working with children!

HARRY ROSS, PH.D., *Associate Professor, National Louis University; Co-author, 13 Steps to Teacher Empowerment*

"The American National Council for the Social Studies defines social studies as "the integrated study of the social sciences and humanities to romote civic competence." Social Studies in the Storytelling Classroom is a unique tool for approaching the standards that prove such competence. Its chapters are vibrant communities populated by unique and diverse stories on a roadmap to socio-cultural literacy. These stories affirm and support the art and heart that lie within social sciences and emphasize what is human in the study of humanities. For this reason the Youth, Educators and Storytellers Alliance (a Special Interest Group of the National Storytelling Network) recommends this book to educators and mentors, as well as to those who would share stories in classrooms, and adds it voice to the voices of humanity with a resounding YES!"

LYN FORD, *storyteller, teaching artist, and YES! Alliance co-chairperson*

"The study of relationships, economics, politics, all the connections that traditional tales give us to everyday life make them invaluable instructional tools for social studies. And it's time to teach social studies again; in this country's race to raise reading and math scores social studies has been woefully neglected."

SUSAN MCCULLOUGH, *school counselor at the Leipzig International School, Leipzig, Germany*

"In today's digital world the case for using storytelling as performed by a living breathing person is expertly explained, presented and realized in the chapters. Too often, we rely on already produced materials online when a folktale ably told to a group of listeners results in understanding, empathy and comprehension of history and culture. Reading the culture chapter with the accompanying lesson plans has inspired me to look at my repertoire of stories to tell and reconsider ways I can include in my sessions to enhance the listeners' experience."

KIRK PALMER, *primary school library media specialist, Singapore American School*

"A remarkably practical book that will help teachers, teaching librarians, and others bring social studies to vibrant life for their students. Highly recommended."

BARBARA WILLIAMS, PH.D., *Adjunct, University of California, Berkeley*

"Imagination, emotion and fact. The connection of these three characteristics through the power of the narrative make social studies come alive for students. They don't merely learn history, they feel history, and in the feeling take part of it for themselves. Stenson and Norfolk provide educators with not only the reasons for the use of narrative in classrooms, but multiple and diverse clear examples of how to achieve these aims. Clear, concise and imaginative lesson plans allow teachers to imagine how their classrooms and their students might be nurtured by the use of narratives and how to achieve this goal."

RICKIE CROWN, PH.D., *Adjunct, National Louis University; Latin Teacher, Baker Demonstration School Emerita*

Social Studies in the Storytelling Classroom

EXPLORING OUR CULTURAL VOICES AND PERSPECTIVES

Jane Stenson and Sherry Norfolk

Parkhurst Brothers, Inc., Publishers
LITTLE ROCK

www.parkhurstbrothers.com

Parkhurst Brothers books are distributed to the trade through the Chicago Distribution Center, and may be ordered through Ingram Book Company, Baker & Taylor, Follett Library Resources and other book industry wholesalers. To order from Chicago's Chicago Distribution Center, phone 1-800-621-2736 or send a fax to 800-621-8476. Copies of this and other Parkhurst Brothers, Inc., Publishers titles are available to organizations and corporations for purchase in quantity by contacting Special Sales Department at our home office location, listed on our web site. Manuscript submission guidelines for this publishing company are available at our web site.

Printed in the United States of America

First Edition, 2012

2012 2013 2014 2015 2016 2017 2018 16 15 14 13 12 11 10 9 8 7 6 5 4 3 2 1

Library of Congress Cataloging in Publication Data:

Stenson, Jane, 1941-
Social studies in the storytelling classroom: cultural perspectives and voices: who tells the story? / Jane Stenson and Sherry Norfolk.
p. cm.
Includes bibliographical references and index.
ISBN 978-1-935166-68-9
1. Social sciences—Study and teaching (Elementary) 2. Storytelling. 3. Interdisciplinary approach in education. I. Norfolk, Sherry, 1952- II. Title.
LB1584.S692 2012
372.83'044—dc23
2012005788

ISBN: Original Trade Paperback 978-1-935166-56-6 [10 digit: 1-935166-56-5]

ISBN: e-book 978-1-935166-57-3 [10-digit: 1-935166-57-3]

This book is printed on archival-quality paper that meets requirements of the American National Standard for Information Sciences, Permanence of Paper, Printed Library Materials, ANSI Z39.48-1984.

Cover Design and Design Director:
Wendell E. Hall

Text Design:
Shelly Culbertson

Acquired for Parkhurst Brothers, Inc., Publishers by:
Ted Parkhurst

Editor:
Sandie Williams

102012

Dedications

To Evan, Zach, and Kate,
children who love to tell and listen to stories,
whose energy, compassion and intelligence
inspire the adults who love and care for them.
—JS

To Bobby,
the man who keeps me laughing, inspires,
consoles, supports, and encourages
me through it all.
You are my SSPTBAFGG—WAO!
— SN

CONTENTS

FOREWORD

Why Stories?

Carmen Agra Deedy

A century ago, the notion that the human species might one day find storytelling obsolete (like some Darwinian limb that has outgrown its usefulness) might have been met with scorn, incredulity, even hilarity.

I don't believe that suggestion would incite much laughter now.

Children, in increasing numbers, are growing up in a world without story. Rare is the family dinner where the day's tales are shared, fewer the working parents who can muster the stamina to tell bedtime stories, far-removed the grandparents who once shared multi-generational homes and were a reliable source of fantastical tales.

For those of us who work with children, this is an alarming evolutionary trend. Why so strong a term? After all, how great would the loss truly be if future generations were to cull their stories from inanimate bits and bytes of technology.

Great indeed, *because although we use machines, we are not machines.*

We are social animals and storytelling is the empathic tie that binds us to one another with bands of steel. It is much more difficult to hate your enemy once you have heard his story.

We are hard-wired for storytelling. This inclination—scratch that, this *need*—to create narrative out of the daily flotsam of human experience has long been considered a crucial part of what defines us as human beings. We don't just spew facts. We frame them within context, add curious digressions, create dialogue...we make a story out of a trip to the Piggly Wiggly.

At least, we once did.

When a child grows up without hearing family stories, she enters adulthood with an incomplete sense of her personal history. This is loss enough. But when a child grows up without hearing folktales and fairytales, she enters adulthood with an imperfect sense of what it means to be a member of the *human family.*

These tales carry deep within them the wit and wisdom of ancient cultures. Most are hundreds—some thousands—of years old. And they are an essential part of a complete education. They teach us how to treat our enemies, fight our monsters, and die with dignity. They teach us how to laugh at our foibles.

They are a child's birthright.

And a most singular heirloom. A story cannot be lost in a fire, washed away by a flood, or left behind in an evacuation. It is an inheritance indestructible.

Or nearly so.

Its survival hangs on one immutable requirement: *a story must be told.*

__CARMEN AGRA DEEDY__ has been writing for over two decades. Born in Havana, Cuba, she came to the U.S. as a refugee in 1964 and grew up in Decatur, Georgia, where she lives today. Deedy began writing as a young mother and storyteller whose NPR (National Public Radio) commentaries on All Things Considered were collected and released under the title Growing Up Cuban in Decatur, Georgia. Carmen's children's books have received many accolades, such as the Jane Addams Peace Association Book Award (Honor), Parent's Choice Gold Award, Bologna Ragazzi Award, Pura Belpre Honor Award, and an ALA (American Library Association) Odyssey Audio Award. They have been translated into dozens of languages, with her most recent children's book, 14 Cows for America becoming a New York Times Bestseller. Having spent years writing and telling stories, Carmen has been an invited speaker at the American Library Association, Refugees International, the International Reading Association, The Smithsonian, TED (Technology Entertainment and Design), the National Book Festival, and the Kennedy Center. However, children remain her favorite audience. Carmen's latest book The Cheshire Cheese Cat was released October 1, 2011.

ACKNOWLEDGEMENTS

We are grateful to...

- Our publisher, Ted Parkhurst, who loves books and admires their authors! Having a responsive and interested publisher makes all the difference. Thanks Ted.
- Shelly Culbertson, whose beautiful design demonstrates her care and understanding of our contributors' work, and provides readers a visual guide through the content. Lovely!
- Lyn Ford, who brought the beautiful adinkra symbols to our attention. We print them courtesy of "West African Wisdom: Adinkra Symbols and Meanings". http://www.adinkras.org
- Jane's neighborly neighbors Josiah and Matty Evans for their timely and expert tech help. When the graphics would not move, they calmly and quickly organized and moved all the little pieces to the proper places, all the while repeating, "Don't worry! It's still there!"
- The amiable and articulate Jonathan Friedman for supremely superb photographs of children's work in the sunshine and in the shade.
- Kevin Strauss for a mind-bending conversation on "The Three Pigs" told at Northlands Conference 2011.
- Susan McCullough, guidance counselor and teacher, who offered us an essay on the clear and present need to reintroduce social studies learning into the schools. Her point was that schools are so hobbled by literacy and math testing that the essence of social studies learning that schools are meant to provide has been side-stepped.
- The faculty and children at the Baker Demonstration School, Wilmette, IL who love and expect good stories to frame their learning and relationships.

NCSS is the National Council for Social Studies which has themes or standards that delineate the content areas for social studies. They graciously allowed our use of the first four standards for this book. Each appears at the beginning of the chapters.

NCSS 1: CULTURE
NCSS 2: TIME, CONTINUITY & CHANGE
NCSS 3: PEOPLE, PLACES & ENVIRONMENT
NCSS 4: IDENTITY & INDIVIDUAL DEVELOPMENT

We are grateful for the use of the following photographs:

- Rock City Photos courtesy of "See Rock City."
- http://www.seerockcity.com/pages/The-Geographic-Wonders-of-Rock-City
- Satchel Paige, Mary Chestnut and Mary Livermore photos courtesy of Wikipedia, the free encyclopedia. File: Satchel Paige.jpg, Mary Livermore, jpeg. Mary Chestnut, jpeg.
- John Herrington, Louise Erdich, Sam Bradford, Tom Cole, Lourriene Roy, Jim Thorpe, Adam Beach photos courtesy of Wikipedia, the free encyclopedia. File: John Herrington, jpeg, Louise Erdich, jpeg, Sam Bradford, jpeg, Tom Cole, jpeg, Lourraine Roy, jpeg, Jim Thorpe, jpeg, Adam Beach, jpeg.
- Photograph No. 210-G-A39 (Photographer Dorothea Lange); "San Francisco, California. Exclusion Order posted at First and Front Streets directing removal of persons of Japanese ancestry from the first San Francisco section to be effected by the evacuation."; Records of the War Relocation Authority, Record Group 210, furnished courtesy of the National Archives at College Park, College Park, MD.
- Photograph No. 210-CC-S (26C) "The Hirano family, left to right, George, Hisa, and Yasbei. Colorado River Relocation Center, Poston, Arizona, 1942 - 1945"; Records of the War Relocation Authority, Record Group 210, furnished courtesy of the National Archives at College Park, College Park, MD.

And, as always, we are humbled by the incredible generosity, talent, and insight of our contributors. To say, "we couldn't have done this without you" is an understatement! Thank you each and every one for sharing your work with other storytellers, teaching artists, and classroom teachers, in the hope that our children will be prepared to "assume the office of citizen" (Seefeldt, 2001) in an ever-changing world.

Seefeldt, Carol. *Social Studies for the Preschool/Primary Child.* (6th ed.) Merrill/Prentice Hall, 2001

ESE NE TEKREMA

"The teeth and the tongue"

Symbol of friendship and interdendence.

The teeth and the tongue play interdependent roles in the mouth.

They may come into conflict, but they need to work together.

Introduction

Jane Stenson

"When the seventh mouse came upon the Something, she ran up one side and she ran down the other. She ran across the top and from end to end. "Ah," said White Mouse. "Now I see. The Something is

as sturdy as a pillar,
as supple as a snake,
as wide as a cliff,
as sharp as a spear,
as breezy as a fan,
as stringy as a rope, but all together the Something is an elephant!"

And when the other mice ran up one side and down the other, across the Something from end to end, they agreed. Now they saw it, too.

The Mouse Moral: Knowing in part may make a fine tale, but wisdom comes from seeing the whole."

Young, Ed. *Seven Blind Mice*, NY: Philomel, 1992.

Exploring the relationship between storytelling and social studies challenges our 21st century selves to pay attention to the folktales and the narrative non-fictions that teach our hearts and minds and to the American voices which call out to be heard. If our social studies goals for children are that they become compassionate citizens, informed and critical thinkers, and committed to social justice, then stories and storytelling are the curriculum of choice. Filmmaker Peter Guber wrote in *Psychology Today* (March 15, 2011) that "stories are the most efficient means of persuasion in everyday life, the most effective way of translating ideas into action." Simultaneously, progressive educator and Stanford education professor Linda Darling-Hammond in addressing Columbia University's Teachers College warns "education must measure its efficiency in terms of increased humanism, increased power to do, increased capacity to appreciate." This is what our book is about: social studies in the storytelling classroom or storytelling in the social studies classroom. Who tells the story? What is the point of view? What and who is the story about? Wisdom comes from seeing the whole.

Our contributors—teachers and storytellers—have written their best essays and articles and have supplied ample activities that address content and skill goals for children in social studies. The variety and breadth of the articles is gladdening—there are many ways to teach social studies! When we think about the role of storytelling in the classroom, it is clear that non-fiction stories are increasingly popular in schools, social studies textbooks, with trade book publishers, and with platform tellers. Non-fiction's ascendance marks a societal shift toward what is quantifiable. "Just the facts, Ma'am." In many places education has shifted into what is measurable. Yet, we know that facts and figures are not easily remembered. One of our authors Elizabeth Ellis says she wants the time back at the end of her life that she spent memorizing information about countries that no longer exist! Having a critical frame that explains why those facts are important is what is often missing.

That means social studies must begin with the folktale and the folksong—the collected wisdom of the people. It is the heart that remembers through sensory frames what it means to feel respected and secure...or not. And, educational theorists explain that imagination, seeing possibilities, and the ability to work with one's peers are skills our citizens need; that social knowledge comes, in the beginning, from the family and the folktale. Whatever the social studies unit, the folktale is the basis for understanding the geography, the cultures, the sweep of history and the identity of the peoples. Or, another thought: we are fighting in the world on many fronts; are we learning the folktales of our "enemies" or only our own stories?

Storytellers know that creating images which provoke metaphoric thought will spur the heart to remember and the mind to understand: The glint of a spur impressed on the heart of four year old Minne allows the listener to recognize that war affects generations of people. (Horner—chapter two)

Teachers know children need a framework plus an activity to understand past and present events; sensory details and simulated events emblazon history on student participants: "Students wait in line to be registered. When they tell you their name, Americanize it, and give them a card with their new name and a number on it. Go to the doctor. The doctor will put a blue mark on your card if you need to be quarantined and a red mark on your card if you are going to be sent home. If your card is unmarked, you will be sent to the American mainland." (Washington—chapter two)

The best social studies learning in this century is about multiple perspectives, analytical thinking, synthesizing ideas, making connections, and always recognizing that the individual develops in a social group. Groups overlap. Social studies is the study of people in social situations in their physical world.

In "Using Story to Understand the Reality of Undocumented Latino Youth" (chapter four) Jim Winship and James Hartwick supply us with the Structured Academic Controversy or SAC method for a complete look at a political and cultural situation and an empathetic approach through collected stories of the people involved in the situation.

Jo Radner takes third through fifth graders on a year long oral history project to document a huge fire in her locality in 1947. What was tragedy in 1947 becomes community affirmation in 2010. (chapter two)

Three articles about the Civil War shed light on the synthesis of storytelling and teaching when teacher Kate Anderson McCarthy and storytellers Syd Lieberman and Beth Horner collaborated to encourage critical thinking for fourth graders. (chapter two)

Teachers Brandi Self and Aya Borchers present the underlying physical bases for peoples' activity (real people and imagined people!) in their articles on the Nez Pierce and tall tales respectively. (chapter three)

Teaching and writing about cultures brings up the enmeshed quality of our multicultural world. People move, change counties and countries, intermarry and have children. All families contain many ethnicities and nationalities; what does it mean to be human and alive in an increasingly diverse and swiftly moving world? We still struggle to 'get along.' The patriarchal ways are leaving—not easily and not quickly—but as The Rev. Dr. Martin Luther King said, "The arc of moral history is long. It bends toward justice."

Looking at preconceived ideas and expectations, Andy Offut Irwin (chapter four) speaks to uncovering and challenging racism through story.

In chapter one Charlotte Blake Alston asks that we dig deeper into our African and African-American proverbs and folktales that they will teach us the oral and cultural tradition…to learn the reality of those cultures.

Bobby Norfolk begins his article "Shadowball" with Satchel Paige's *"Ain't no man can avoid being born average, but there ain't no man got to be common."*

That's right, Satchel! We call on school children, their teachers and families and storytellers to be their best selves, especially in social situations. By seeking contributors who articulate the NCSS standards for Culture, History, Geography and Identity we have put together our hopes for ways that social studies can re-enter America's schools to the benefit of our communities, the nation and the world.

> "We can bring warmth into places where young persons come together…we can bring in the dialogues and laughter that threaten monologues and rigidity. And surely we can affirm and reaffirm the principles that center around belief in justice and freedom and respect for human rights, since without these, we cannot even call for the decency of welcoming and inclusion for everyone, no matter how at risk. Only if more and more persons in their coming together learn to incarnate such principles and choose to live and speak in accord with them, are we likely to bring a community into being. All we can do is speak with others as passionately and eloquently as we can; all we can do is to look into each other's eyes and urge each other on to new beginnings. Our classrooms ought to be nurturing and thoughtful and just all at once; they ought to pulsate with multiple conceptions of what it is to be human and alive. They ought to resound with the voices of articulate young people in dialogues always incomplete because there is always more to be discovered and more to be said. We must want our students to achieve friendship as each one stirs to wide-awakeness, to imaginative action, and to renewed consciousness of possibility." Maxine Greene, *Releasing the Imagination: Essays on Education, the Arts, and Social Change.* San Francisco, CA: Jossey-Bass Education, 2000.

Sankofa is both a proverb and a pictographic, ideographic reminder of the importance of wisdom and heritage. Its pictograph can be the shape of a heart, often designed with extensions that seem to be roots.

CHAPTER ONE

National Council of Social Studies 1. Culture

Social studies programs should include experiences that provide for the study of culture and cultural diversity.

Human beings create, learn, share, and adapt to culture.

Cultures are dynamic and change over time.

Through experience, observation, and reflection, students will identify elements of culture as well as similarities and differences among cultural groups across time and place.

In schools this theme typically appears in units and courses dealing with geography, history, sociology, and anthropology, as well as multicultural topics across the curriculum.

ANNE SHIMOJIMA | ELIZABETH ELLIS
WILLY CLAFLIN | NOA BAUM
CHARLOTTE BLAKE ALSTON | TIM TINGLE

Hana's Suitcase

A STORY TO BRIDGE CULTURES

Anne Shimojima

Several years ago, I was given a book, a story that connects the Holocaust in World War II Europe with modern day Japan. As a Japanese-American storyteller, I was immediately intrigued. The book is *Hana's Suitcase: A True Story* by Karen Levine (Second Story Press, 2002), and my work with this story, with the permission of the author and publisher, has deepened my understanding of the darkest days of the war while it restored my hope in the promise of peace in our world.

During the winter of 2000, Fumiko Ishioka, the director of the Tokyo Holocaust Education Resource Center, received several artifacts from the Auschwitz concentration camp, including a plain, brown suitcase. On one side of the suitcase, written in white paint, were the words Hana Brady, May 16, 1931, and one word in German, *Waisenkind,* which means "orphan."

The children who volunteered at the center were intrigued by the suitcase. They wanted to know who this mysterious girl could be. Where did she come from? What did she look like? What happened to her that caused her name to be put on the side of a suitcase from a concentration camp? Fumiko promised to try to find out who she was. An inquiry to the Auschwitz museum turned up Hana's name on a list of prisoners from Theresienstadt, the Nazi German ghetto in Czechoslovakia. From the Terezin Ghetto Museum Fumiko received photographs of five pictures drawn by Hana during her time in Theresienstadt.

Meanwhile, the children at the center were writing poems and newsletters about the suitcase and the search for Hana Brady. Eventually, Fumiko was able to travel to the Terezin Ghetto Museum, but only had one day to visit—a day the museum was closed. With the help of a kind staff member who let her in, she found out that Hana had died in Auschwitz but an older brother, George, had survived. At the Jewish Museum in Prague she was put in touch with a man who turned out to be George Brady's bunkmate at Theresienstadt. He provided George's current address in Canada.

It was through George that Fumiko finally discovered Hana's story. Hana lived in Nove Mesto, Czechoslovakia with her father, mother, and George. She was only seven years old in 1939 when the Nazis took over. We learn of the restrictions on Jews and the hardships of their daily life, including the 1940 announcement that Jewish children could no longer attend school, destroying Hana's dream of becoming a teacher.

In 1941, Hana and George's father and mother were both imprisoned, leaving the children in the care of their aunt and uncle. In 1942 the children were sent to Theresienstadt. Hana lived in a girls' dormitory, doing chores and attending secret classes in art and music. In 1944 both George and Hana were sent to Auschwitz. George survived. Hana did not.

When Fumiko wrote to George, she was afraid of stirring up painful memories, but George welcomed the chance to tell about his sister. He sent back a long letter and included photographs of Hana and their family, and in the book we see a clear-eyed, pretty young girl, skiing, ice skating, helping her mother, and posing with her brother and the family wolfhound. We see the hearts made of bread that her mother sent to Hana from Ravensbruck, a women's concentration camp in Germany. We see a yellow star like the ones they were forced to wear on their coats.

In reading about Hana and her suitcase we are introduced to several enmeshed cultures. Hana's Czechoslovakian family feasts on turkey, sausage, salami, and pudding for New Year's Eve, and plays a traditional walnut game. She and George help their parents in their general store by weighing spices, slicing yeast, and cutting lumps off the sugar loaf. Although the Brady family was not very religious, Mr. and Mrs. Brady make sure that George and Hana learn about Jewish history and holidays. Readers will also recognize ways in which the Brady's lives are similar to theirs. Hana and George love their two cats and dog, study the violin and piano, play in the creek behind their house, and build snow forts in the winter.

But when the Nazis take over their town and Nazi culture is forced upon them, we get a glimpse of what it must have been like to live as a Jew during this impossible time. They must turn in their radios, wear yellow stars, and shop only in designated stores during certain hours. They cannot travel, skate on the pond, or use playgrounds, sports fields, parks, or gyms. They cannot leave their home except during certain hours. Other families would not let their children play with Jewish children and Hana loses her best friend. After Mr. and Mrs. Brady are imprisoned, we journey with Hana and George to Theresienstadt and on the train to Auschwitz.

Perhaps the Japanese children identified with Hana's story because it reflected some of their own cultural values. The children urged Fumiko not to give up, to continue her search, which she did through setback after setback, which was reminiscent of *gaman*, the ideal of perseverance. George's lasting regret that he could not save his little sister was an embodiment of *giri*, the principle of duty and obligation. Finally, the Brady family's stoic struggle to survive through their hardships recalls the principle of *shikata ga nai*, or holding on to dignity even in situations beyond one's control.

We can see, too, the universal values that cross many cultures—love of family, the cherishing of children, a belief in education to make a better world, and the dignity of every human being. We are challenged to consider questions: How should we treat people of a different religion? How can we survive in the face of unbearable hardship? How can we forgive? How can we work for peace?

Teaching students about historical events and different cultures is challenging, because the times and the locales may be very far away. But through story, we can enter into the life of one person or one family. It is the story that has drawn us into the world of war-torn Czechoslovakia and that leads us to see through the eyes of a Jewish child. It is the story that helps us to follow the trail of clues that leads Fumiko to unravel the mystery of Hana Brady and how her suitcase came to rest in a Japanese Holocaust center. It is the story that shows us the perseverance and compassion of Japanese children who wondered about a little girl who lived and died so long ago. These children learned about the horrors of war and became dedicated to the advancement of peace in our world, a world where even children can make a difference. And in perhaps the most moving part of the story, George has traveled to the Tokyo Holocaust Education Resource Center to see his sister's suitcase for the first time in over fifty years, and he realizes that one of Hana's dreams has come true. Hana has become a teacher. Through her suitcase and her story thousands of Japanese children were learning about the horrors of the Holocaust. They were learning about tolerance, compassion, and respect.

I was first drawn to this story because of its Japanese connection, of course, and because of my relationships with so many Jewish people—my good friends, my professional colleagues in the schools where I worked, and the thousands of students that I taught. But its humanity and inspiration make it a universal story of endurance and hope for all people.

When I told the story of Hana's suitcase in a storytelling festival several years ago, an older woman identified herself as a Holocaust survivor and she thanked me for telling the story. She told me that I was brave to do so. I told her, no, the really courageous people were the ones who lived the story. It was my honor and privilege to bear witness to it.

The book *Hana's Suitcase* won the Canadian Library Association's Book of the Year Award and numerous other awards. It has been translated into over 40 languages, has been made into a play and a documentary film, and has inspired millions of children and adults around the world. http://www.hanassuitcase.ca/

Levine, Karen. *Hana's Suitcase: A True Story.* Second Story Press, 2002.

***ANNE SHIMOJIMA**, an elementary school library media specialist for thirty-five years, now regularly performs in festivals, schools, libraries, conferences, and museums. In 2001 she appeared at the Exchange Place at the National Storytelling Festival. Anne gives workshops on the use of storytelling in education and on the creation of family history projects. Her World War II family incarceration camp story is available at www.raceridges.com with a lesson plan and discussion questions. www.anneshimojima.com.*

Folktales

OF THE PEOPLE, BY THE PEOPLE, AND FOR THE PEOPLE

Elizabeth Ellis

Democracy is government "of the people, by the people and for the people." The folktale is literature "of the people, by the people and for the people." As such, the folktale is a powerful tool for teaching students about their own culture and that of others, which is a necessary foundation for effective participation in a diverse society.

I grew up in the Appalachian Mountains. Everyone there was exactly the same: one hundred per cent WASP. Diversity in my childhood meant were you a "sprinkler" or a "dunker," beliefs about baptism being the major difference between people. I was in high school when I met the first person I knew was a Catholic. I remember thinking of her as being exotic.

That may not sound like good preparation for living as an adult in a huge multi-cultural city, working with people of a wide variety of religions and ethnicities. My childhood, however, was deeply saturated in folktales. Because of that, I understood who I was and accepted that I came from a culture of strong and independent people. I respected the culture that had created me, and through the beauty and power of folktales, I had learned to honor it. Because I understood and respected the culture that I came from, it was easy to afford the same respect to the culture of others, no matter how different from my own.

I want to make clear that the first step in teaching diversity effectively is to teach an understanding and acceptance of the student's own culture. Far too often diversity means teaching about the cultures of others before the student has developed an understanding of the culture from which he comes. That step is foundational. A child who has not developed a healthy respect for his own culture is not likely to develop respect for the culture of others. Respect, like charity, begins at home.

Understanding cultural diversity is actually a three-step process. The first step is accepting that everyone comes from a culture, and that they are entitled to express that culture. It is an essential part of their humanity and "an inalienable right." It is in this step that we recognize we are more alike than we are different. The second step is to learn to respect the culture of others, even though it may be different from your own. An essential part of this step is learning that the expression of their culture does not in any way threaten or demean your own. In this step we begin to understand the differences that make up individual cultures. The third and highest step is learning to honor the culture of others, to find delight in both the similarities and the differences. It is in this step that we learn to celebrate diversity as a strength of human life. The folktale has the unique ability to meet the needs of students in each of these three steps.

This is no idealistic "edu-babble." Our students will be voting citizens of a multi-cultural democracy; they must be capable of understanding larger and more complex issues than their ancestors. (Pink, 2006) Understanding that there is more than one point of view on an issue has never been more important. Respect for the opinions of others is one of the foundations of our democracy. Our students must also be prepared to make a positive economic contribution to the world in which they will live. That part is essential for our national security. Remember, most people do not get fired because they are unable to do the work, but because they are unable to get along with their co-workers.

Unfortunately, our knowledge of folktales has been diminished over the years. When we hear the term "folktale," we tend to think "Cinderella," or perhaps "The Threes: Bears, Pigs and Billy Goats." Contemporary children do not know many folktales past these. In fact, they are more likely to know mangled adaptations than the stories those parodies are based upon. Folktale is a huge body of lore that includes, but is not limited to the tall tale, the trickster story, the fairy tale, the pourquoi or how and why tale, the legend, the ghost story, the wisdom story or teaching tale, the fable, the myth, the noodle head story, the circle story, the chain story. There are stories of each of these types from every culture around the world. So there is never any shortage of material with which to work. There is truly something appropriate for every stage of a child's development.

The folktale is the cornerstone of understanding any cultural heritage. Within the simple framework of story, we come to understand the basics of the culture which produced the tale. What is the basic family structure? What is the way of life of this people? What is their relationship to the world in which they live? How are people in relationship to one another? What is their relationship to Spirit? These questions form foundational cultural literacy for the understanding of culture—our own, and that of others— on which all effective teaching of social studies is built.

In the folktale, we come to accept that we are much the same. People love their family members, even if the family is structured differently from our own. People have the same needs. Those go beyond food, clothing and shelter. People want to be loved, respected and treated fairly. They want meaning in their lives and are willing to take risks to have it. (Shannon, 1992) Within the folktale we find universal themes and symbols (Hamilton, 2005) that speak to us at our deep heart's core. Who has not felt as put upon as Cinderella? Or as betrayed as Hansel and Gretel? And who has not desperately desired three wishes? Hearing variants from other cultures cements in us the similarities of the human condition. We are also able to hear the differences in other cultures in a non-threatening and non-judgmental way. We learn to respect the differences between us and others. The acceptance of differences may even be integral to the story itself. In folktales, it is often the one who is seen as the "other" who has the needed information or offers the necessary aid. The old ugly woman at the side of the road, when listened to, has the essential gift "for your time of greatest need." The youngest son, seen by his family as a fool, is the one humble enough to follow instruction, and is, therefore, successful on his quest.

These stories are filled with symbols of lasting meaning, strong enough to be adapted to the needs of the listener no matter what the story's origin. Carpets that can fly, combs that become forests, the cloak of invisibility: these are durable symbols and easily adapted to the current needs of the listeners.

Stories are not good because they are old. They are old because they are good. Folktales come from the people. People change. Every time the consciousness of a people changes, the stories that they tell change. It happens naturally. People often ask me, "How many stories do you know?" I say, "About four hundred." Growing up in the South in the late '40s and '50s, I remember well the signs over the water fountains. No one has ever asked me how many of the stories I heard as a child I would be willing to tell in a public place. Stories change as people change. That happens all the time all over the world.

A caution: this change should happen naturally and at the hands of the people who produced the story. There is always the desire to change the folktale to make it fit modern and Western sensibilities. We want to take out all the violence. We want to whitewash anything in the story that might be disturbing. We want to universalize a story to make it more acceptable or understandable. Often in doing that, we rob the story of the power to do its intended work. A story is like medicine. To do its work, it must be administered undiluted. Violence is a part of children's natural lives. Children hunger for justice. Evil must be punished, not excused. The disturbing story is often the one with the power to heal children's deepest wounds. Removing from the story everything that does not conform to our culture's sensibilities robs students of a true understanding of the culture from which the story comes. Omitting from the story that the king has many sons because he has many wives may be a quick fix for a potential question from the children, but does not serve them as citizens of a continually shrinking world.

Often people avoid sharing folktales with students because they are concerned about the presence of ghosts, monsters, witches and other subjects that might be scary. Of course, they are scary. They are meant to be. (Livo, 1994) The scary story is the way children learn to face their fears in a safe and protected environment. These stories have been the way adults have given children a chance to encounter fear in a safe and protected environment and learn to master it in an age appropriate way. Children like to hear the same stories again and again until they have mastered whatever there was in that story that attracted them to it. Once they have reached that mastery, they are no longer interested in hearing that previously favorite story any more. Instead, they want to move on to stories that will give them opportunity to learn how to grapple with their most current fears. There are lots of things in this world that are well worth being afraid of. A child who grows up not hearing scary stories is ill equipped to live in the real world because they have not had a strong and varied background of scary stories to give them experience in dealing with their fears. They have a tendency to grow up afraid of everything and unable to cope with those fears.

Literary stories are often beautiful, but they are the product of the author. They represent the wisdom and insight of one individual. Not so the folktale. A folktale is a story that has been handed down by word of mouth over many generations. It is the product of the wisdom and insight of an entire people, an entire culture. From time out of mind, the older generation has used the folktale to teach the younger generation what their culture values, what is appropriate behavior. Look closely at any folktale, no matter how simple the story may be, and you will begin to see what the culture that produced the story values. Think of a story as simple as "The Little Red

Hen." We all heard it in kindergarten. It is fun to tell and to hear, but twined deeply into the story is a teaching that is basic to our American culture—"He who does not work will not eat." In this simple nursery tale from our culture you hear the echo of the economist Adam Smith and The Wealth of Nations as well as Ralph Waldo Emerson's essay on "Self Reliance."

An understanding of what is considered acceptable behavior in any culture is basic to the teaching of social studies. All social studies teaching must include teaching character to prepare students to live in their world as actualized adults and productive, participating citizens.

I want returned to me at the end of my life all the time I spent learning facts about countries that no longer exist! The teaching of social studies must include more than factual information. Most children can regurgitate the facts. More is needed from our citizenry than that. Critical thinkers are essential to our national security. The importance of discourse cannot be underestimated, either. Every child must have a voice at the table. And every child must understand the importance of their voice and the need for respect for the voices of others. An effective social studies classroom will teach the necessity of the true sharing of ideas. The group will always know more than the individual knows.

We need to move from the "Little Bird" model, where we expect to pour knowledge into the mouths of students, to a model that embraces the importance of teacher as facilitator of understanding. How to find the question is as important as how to find the answer. How to work with others is the most important understanding of all.

RESOURCES

"Eleven Cinderellas" Hamilton, Mary. *Sisters All...and One Troll.* CD. Frankfort, KY: Hidden Spring, 2005.

Livo, Norma. *Who's Afraid...? Facing Children's Fears With Folktales.* Englewood, CO: Libraries Unlimited, 1994.

Pink, Daniel H. *A Whole New Mind: Why Right-Brainers Will Rule the Future.* "Story", pp. 100-128. New York: Riverhead Books, 2005.

Shannon, George. *A Knock At the Door.* Westport, CT: The Oryx Multicultural Folktale Series, Greenwood Publishing Group, 1992. And others in this series.

OBJECTIVES *for Grade Three*

Students will

- learn that all cultures at one time transmitted their collective knowledge orally, and some cultures still do today.
- understand how the folktale is passed down by word of mouth from generation to generation by participation in a "family".
- examine similarities between cultures, as well as differences.
- observe how oral literature influences written literature and helps to shape it.

MATERIALS

Gather a number of folktales from different cultures, which have Rabbit as the Trickster: Br'er Rabbit, Tio Conejo, Rabbit from the Southeast Indian tribes. We will use "The Tortoise and the Hare" from Aesop's Fables, understanding that these fables did not originate but passed into the Anglo oral tradition hundreds of years ago.

Some examples

- NATIVE AMERICAN

  Ross, Gayle. *How Rabbit Tricked Otter and Other Cherokee Trickster Stories.* New York: Parabola Books, 2003.

  Scheer, George. *Cherokee Animal Tales.* New York: Holiday, 1968.

- AFRICAN AMERICAN

  Courlander, Harold. *Terrapin's Pot of Sense.* New York: Holt, 1957.

  Harris, Joel Chandler. Adapted by Parks, Van Dyke and Jones, Malcolm. *Jump! The Adventures of Brer Rabbit.* New York: Harcourt, Brace, Jovanovich, Publishers, 1986.

- HISPANIC

  Loya, Olga. *Tio Conejo (Uncle Rabbit) and Other Latin American Trickster Tales.* Little Rock, AR: August House Publishers, 2006.

  Loya, Olga. *Momentos Magicos/Magic Moments.* Little Rock, AR: August House, 1997.

  Belpré, Pura. *Tiger and Rabbit and other Tales.* Philadelphia, PA: Lippincott, 1965.

- ANGLO-AESOP [Recognizing that Aesop's tales have passed into the Anglo oral tradition]
  Aesop's Fables. New York: Watts, 1968.
- JAPANESE
  Ozaki, Yei Theodora. *Japanese Fairy Book.* New York: Dover, 1967. Contains a story of Hare tricking Badger into making a boat of mud that sinks.
- KOREAN
  Kim, So-Un. *The Story Bag: A Collection of Korean Folktales.* Rutland, VT: Tuttle, 1955. Contains a story of Hare tricking Tiger.

You will also want a copy of

- Potter, Beatrix. *The Tale of Peter Rabbit.* London: Warne, 1903.

INSTRUCTIONAL PLAN

1. Teacher (or storyteller) learns to tell at least one story about Rabbit as Trickster from each of the cultures listed above. The easiest way to do this is to read the story a few times and then make a storyboard. Draw a picture of each major thing that happens in the story. Begin telling the story to yourself using the storyboard as a visual outline. After a few self-tellings, you will be ready to share the stories with your students. The stories are simple and easy to learn to tell. Don't panic. It won't take as long as you think!
2. Divide the students into "families." Each family will have a grandparent," a "parent," a "child," a "grandchild" and a "great grandchild." The size and structure of the "families" will depend on the number of students in the class.
3. Discuss with your students the meaning of "oral tradition." Ask them to think through learning everything they know orally.
4. Acting as the "ancestor," tell one of the stories you have learned to the grandparent in one of the "families". Impress upon the student that he will be passing the story on to the parent in his group and must remember as much of the story as possible. Repeat any parts of the story, if asked. The grandparent will repeat the story to the ancestor to make sure the story is learned and understood.

5. Tell a different story to each of the grandparents.
6. The grandparent tells the story to the parent. The parent repeats the story to the grandparent to ensure it has been learned and understood. This process is repeated throughout the family group.
7. A more meaningful discussion of "oral culture" may take place now. Students will have a framework for understanding passing on information without the intervention of print or media. Discuss "passed down by word of mouth."
8. The great grandchild in each family will tell the story to the "village" of families in the classroom. They will be assisted in this task by their family members who were responsible for teaching them the story that is to be shared with the village.

ASSESSMENT

Family members go to other classrooms to share their story. Each storyteller is accompanied by a family member whose role is to report whether the story was shared accurately. The objective of the work is to understand the oral tradition within a culture. The telling of a story passed through several "generations" of students demonstrates this.

ANOTHER STEP

Ask each family to generate a list of the things they have learned about the folktale character Rabbit. Ask each family to share their list. Discuss how is he the same in each culture? How is he different in each culture?

Read *The Tale of Peter Rabbit* by Beatrix Potter to the students.

- Discuss how Beatrix Potter's character, Peter Rabbit is like Br'er Rabbit, Tio Conejo, etc., and how he is different.
- Discuss how a writer draws on folktales and how they influence a writer's work.

ASSESSMENT

Ask the students to write an original story using one of the Rabbit characters they have studied.

Appalachian born ***ELIZABETH ELLIS*** *has shared her special brand of literary magic with more than a million school children for more than thirty years. She is a recipient of the Circle of Excellence Award from the National Storytelling Network and the John Henry Faulk Award from the Tejas Storytelling Association. A respected teacher of storytellers, Elizabeth conducts weekend intensives and workshops for teller growth and renewal. With Loren Niemi, Elizabeth co-authored the award winning book,* ***Inviting the Wolf In: Thinking About Difficult Stories.*** *www.elizabethellis.com*

Time Capsules

OLD BALLADS IN THE MODERN CLASSROOM

Willy Claflin

"Lord Bangam rode to the wild boar's den,
There he spied the bones of a hundred men.
Derum-kimmie-quo-qua!"

Singing old ballads in the classroom is a kind of time travel. I often turn off the fluorescent lights, just to remind everyone that we're going back to a time and place before electricity. We're entering a realm where there are no microphones, no recordings, no way to broadcast anything. In short, we move to the world that existed for 99% of human history; where most people cannot read or write, and rhyming and remembering are survival skills.

This world can seem alien to children in the current age. It can also fascinate them. Ballads and folk songs are like time capsules; windows into other worlds. When students can learn them, sing them, they're rewarded with a deeper understanding of cultures and eras far removed from their own.

As a visiting artist, I've done ballad units with junior high and high school students (ages 12 to 18). Much of the material presented in this article would not be appropriate for students in grades K-5. But hundreds of traditional story-songs exist which are just right for younger listeners, and I hope that many of the observations and activities that follow will also be useful to teachers in the primary grades.

What is a ballad, anyway?

This is a good question to begin with. The most common modern definition is a slow, sentimental song, probably a love song. I asked this question in a 7th grade classroom, and a boy got up and did a very entertaining sappy ballad: "When I hold you, darling, in my arms, all the angels in Heaven sing..." he crooned. Everybody laughed, and we were off to a great start. Then we looked the word up, and found out that there were two definitions, and that the first one ("the old one" the kids rightfully called it) meant a narrative song. After a brief discussion, the students defined this as "a song that tells a story," and I think this is just as good a working definition as any.

If I have only one or two classes to investigate the subject, I do a mini-survey from my own Scots-Irish-English tradition, presenting and discussing a dozen songs—from the 16th century to the present day. We begin in Scotland in the 1500s, and end in present day America. In the process, we trace the Scots-Irish migration into Appalachia, the westward expansion, American heroes and hard cases, dust bowl days, protest songs and political broadsides.

Most of what follows here is a sampling of narrative ballads, with suggested topics for classroom discussion. At the end, I've added a short list of recommended class activities and projects.

My first goal is simple exposure: I sing the songs in the traditional style, and answer student questions. And as interesting as it is to analyze these songs, to derive clues about their societal context, I remind myself that it's even more important to sing them, and hear them sung.

So—I begin by singing a song or two. Almost always a cappella, the way the old ballads were sung. I realize that not everyone is comfortable singing. But I would suggest that you just set that aside, and teach yourself an old ballad to sing, one that's relevant to a social studies unit you're working on. Remember, we're talking about folk music here—that is, music that ordinary folks sing. The point of ballads is to tell a story, not necessarily to sing on pitch!

For teachers who are particularly reluctant to sing, there are a few options:

1. Ask your music teacher to learn and sing a couple of ballads for the class.
2. Check out traditional musicians in your area—you'll likely find local folks who would enjoy coming in and sharing a few songs.
3. Check out CDs and downloads by the musicians listed at the end of this article.
4. With the rapid ascent of YouTube, you can often find several versions of traditional ballads online, and present them to your class that way.

But bear in mind: nothing beats in-person, face-to-face live presentation of this material—it's part of what helps us understand its meaning, part of what helps us truly travel back in time. And we all know that the best way to teach something is to model it yourself!

Older students sometimes have a prejudice against what they think of as 'folk music.' And so, I like to point out before I begin, both as a warning and an enticement, that the most ancient songs are usually filled with murder, mystery and mayhem; that despite parental worry about hip hop lyrics, the old ballads have an even higher incidence of violence in them. In a way, the old ballads were the tabloids, the TV crime shows of their day. And I've found that, especially with boys in grades seven to twelve, the promise of "bloody ballads" is a good way to get their attention.

And so I might begin by singing the 17th century Scottish ballad "The Rose and The Lindsy-O" (also known as "The Cruel Mother.")

There was a king's daughter, lived in the north,
Aye the rose, and the lindsy-o
And she was courted by her father's clark
Awa by the greenwood sidey-o.
She's leaned her back against the thorn,
Aye the rose, and the lindsy-o
And there her twa bonny boys were born,
She's taken out her little pen knife
And there she has taken her bonny boys' life,
One day when she was in the hall
She saw twa bonny boys playing at the ball
"Oh little boys, if you was mine
I'd dress you up in silk so fine."
"Oh, mother dear, when we were thine,
You dressed us not in silk so fine."
"Oh little boys, come tell to me,
Tell me, tell me, what death I'll die."
"You'll be seven long years a bird in the wood,
And seven long years a fish in the flood.
"And for seven years hear a warning bell,
And seven years at the gates of hell."
"Oh, it's welcome, welcome, bird in the wood
And welcome, welcome, fish in the flood.
And welcome, welcome, warning bell,
But the God in Heaven keep me out of hell!"

I've kept track of initial student reactions I've heard over the years. A brief sample: "Weird!" "Gross—she stabbed her kids!" "That was cool!" "What happened?" "Sing it again!" "I don't get it—how could she turn into a bird?" "What's a Lindsy-O?" "Like, those were her kids—who were dead?" "How come she killed them?"

Ballad discussions can begin anywhere. But I usually try to steer them with questions like:

1. What do you notice about the language? Are there words that you don't understand; that don't seem familiar? What do they mean? What does "flood" mean here? "Bonny?"
2. The word "clark" here means "clerk." Why did the king have a clerk? What did the clerk do? Could the king read and write?
3. Why does the king's daughter kill her children? What's the motive?
4. She asks the ghosts of her little boys what death she'll die. Will she really morph into a bird? a fish? Did people in the 1600s believe that could happen?
5. Think of this song as a time capsule. Based only on the words of the song, what can you tell about the world at the time the song was written?
6. Why does the song have a repeating nonsense refrain?
7. Who would the audience have been for this tune? Where would it have been sung?

In discussing questions like these, the world of 17th century Scotland begins to open to us in a very interesting way.

Here, in brief, are a few more suggestions for traditional ballads from the British Isles. The lyrics are all easily available online, and I won't take up space reprinting them here.

"Lord Bangam" (also known as Sir Lionel): This is a straightforward adventure ballad—Lord Bangam wins the maiden by slaying the wild boar. It has a most mysterious nonsense refrain.

Possible topics for discussion: What's the weird refrain mean? Where might it have come from? Is a wild boar just a wild pig? Were they really all that dangerous?

"Nottamun Town": A 16th century mummers' tune, with mysterious dreamlike lyrics: "Sat down on a hard, hot cold frozen stone/ten thousand stood around me, and yet I's alone/put my hat in my hands, for to keep my head warm/ten thousand got drownded that never was born."

Discussion: What were (are) mummers? What does this song mean? Where would it have been sung? Is it just nonsense? How does it make you feel?

"Tamlin": This is a great story and an excellent listening exercise. Young Tamlin is kidnapped by the Queen of Elvinland, and rescued by Lady Margaret. Full length versions are about ten minutes long, so it can be a listening challenge. Suggest that students imagine it as a movie, with a series of scenes. And while listening to this, or any of the longer ballads (and some have up to 50 verses), it's useful to imagine the world in which they were made up and sung. Dim light—a fire or lantern perhaps, shadows on the wall. Folks gathered at a family hearth, or an inn. And as the song—the story set to music—is sung, everyone has his or her own private movie playing in their heads.

This particular song has led to interesting discussions about "how do you remember all of that?" It's good to remind students that before memory was outsourced to the Cloud, folks often developed prodigious powers of memorizing. A typical traditional performer of song and story, even today, probably has at least 12 hours of material memorized, ready to pull out at any moment. It's good to point out that in traditional societies most of the folks couldn't read or write, so memorization was extremely important.

Ballads in American History

American history units are always enlivened by the introduction of traditional ballads. Here's a sample of story-songs that have proved popular with older students over the years:

"Buffalo Skinners": Sometimes I sing the song first and then ask the kids what they can tell me about the country at that point in time, based only on the lyrics. Sometimes I set the song in context, telling the students the following: In the late 1700s, there were 50 million buffalo on the Great Plains. By the late 1800s, there were only 400 left. Millions were shot for profit. Millions were shot at the order of the federal government, in an attempt to destroy the Plains Indians by eliminating their main source of food and shelter. And millions were shot for "sport" from the windows of trains. Buffalo hunting was finally outlawed in the 1890s, just in time to save the remnants of the last herd.

The author of these words is unknown. Woody Guthrie later set it to the tune of "The Blind Fiddler."

"It was in the town of Jacksboro, it the year or '73,
A man by the name of Krego came stepping up to me;
He said, how do you do, young fellow, and how'd you like to go
And spend the summer pleasant on the range of the buffalo?"

There isn't enough space to reprint all the lyrics here, but the saga is a grim one. Ten or twelve 'able-bodied' men set out to work for Krego. But the working conditions are worse than awful, and in the end:

"The season being near over, old Krego, he did say:
'You boys done been extravagant, you drank up all your pay.'
We begged him and we pleaded, but still he answered 'No.'
So we left old Krego's bones to bleach, on the range of the buffalo.
And now we've crossed Pease River, boys, and homeward we are bound.
No more in that hellfire country shall ever we be found,
Go home to our wives and sweethearts; tell others not to go
For God's forsaken the buffalo range, and the damned old buffalo."

QUESTIONS FOR DISCUSSION

1. Just looking at the words of this ballad—what can you tell us about American life at the time it was written?
2. American ballads are usually about common people. Older ballads from the British Isles are always about kings, queens, nobles and lords. Why are American ballads about average everyday people instead?
3. Like many young men, the narrator set out west to seek his fortune. When he came back, why did he write a song about it, instead of just telling people?
4. How come he admits that they killed Krego? Isn't he worried that if he sings the song, people will arrest him? If not, why not?

A few more suggestions of American ballads to sing and study:

- "Diamond Joe":
  "Well, I tried three times to quit him, boys, but he did argue so.
  That I'm still punching cattle in the pay of Diamond Joe.
  And when I'm called up yonder, and it's my time to go,
  Give my blankets to my buddies, give my fleas to Diamond Joe."
- "John Henry":
  The legend of John Henry offers ample opportunity to study the difference between history and legend. I recommend Steel Driving Man, by Scott Reynolds Nelson, as an introduction to the actual railroad working conditions in the 1870s and 80s, and the conscripted labor of young black men after the Emancipation.
- "Hell-Bound Train":
  The coming of the railroads gave birth to hundreds of train songs. Some lines even ran to Heaven (or, in this case, to Hell!)

Finally there are the "modern" ballads, whose authors we know. These songs usually deal with current events. There are political broadside ballads, war protest ballads and modern historical ballads. Here are three particularly interesting examples:

- "Pretty Boy Floyd" (Woody Guthrie): Woody turns one of America's most wanted men into a Robin Hood type of folk hero.

  Discussion:
  Who was Pretty Boy, really? Is Woody's song a reliable account of his life? Is there truth in it anyway? How do we ever know if the singer (or the historian, the history book!) is telling us the truth? Is history something definite that happened, or does truth depend on your point of view?

- "Penny Evans" (Steve Goodman): Goodman takes the melody from an old pirate ballad (Flying Cloud) and turns it into a devastating anti-war song.

  Discussion:
  Think about this verse:
  "Oh, my name is Penny Evans, and I just turned twenty one
  A young widow from the war that's being fought in Vietnam,
  And I have two infant daughters, I thank God I have no son;
  Now they say the war is over, but I think it's just begun."

Discussion:
What does she mean, "I think it's just begun?"

- "Rosa Parks" (Neville Brothers): This song tells the story of Rosa Parks, Martin Luther King and the Montgomery bus boycott.

  Sample verse:
  "Now Sister Rose, she was tired, after a hard day on the job
  And all she wanted was a well-deserved rest,
  not a scene from an angry mob.
  The bus driver said, "Move on back,
  'cause a white person wants your seat!"
  But Rose said, 'No—not no more—
  I'm gonna stay here and rest my feet.'"

  Discussion:
  This song is half rap and half ballad. What do you think about combining the two? Would you like the song better if it was all rap? All singing? Can a ballad be a rap? Can a rap be a ballad?

OBJECTIVES *for Grades Six – Twelve*

Students will:

- Hear and discuss a variety of ballads.
- Understand the function and cultural significance of ballads.
- Learn and perform or write and perform a ballad.

INSTRUCTIONAL ACTIVITIES

1. Each student chooses a ballad to research and memorize. Everyone takes a turn giving an oral presentation to the class. This includes background information about the song, and a performance of the ballad itself. Children who are unwilling or unable to sing may choose to recite their ballad from memory, and then play a musical version from a CD or download.

2. Students write (and perform) their own original ballads about an historical event, and set the lyrics to the tune of a ballad they already know. (This has always been a common practice among balladeers, and has the advantage of making sure the students' lyrics fit into a traditional form.) And again, everyone takes a turn presenting to the class.

3. Students write and perform a ballad from their own personal experience, about something that happened to them. (It's sometimes actually easier for children to start with this exercise, as it gives them leeway to write comic lyrics if they choose.)

ASSESSMENT

Original ballads can be assessed on their conformation to ballad format; performance assessments include creativity and effort, and degree of familiarity with material. Students should be asked to provide a factual statement of the event being ballad-ed which reflects research and consideration of the culture the ballad portrays.

RESOURCES

These days, it's often easiest to just Google your subject and see what comes up: songs of the American West, for instance, or American railroad ballads, etc.

Then, there are the hundreds of traditional ballads gathered by the great collectors, all available online:

- Francis James Child (British Isles)
- Cecil Sharpe (British Isles and Appalachia)
- John and Alan Lomax (USA)

And finally, there are the singers and ballad writers, all of whom can be seen and heard online, in addition to offering a wealth of audio recordings.

Here are just a few suggestions:

- ENGLAND/SCOTLAND
  Ewan MacColl, Martin Carthy, Maddie Prior, June Tabor, The Watersons, Archie Fisher; and for traditional folk-rock: Steeleye Span and Fairport Convention.
- USA
  Woody Guthrie, Pete Seeger, Sheila Kay Adams, Jean Ritchie, Peggy Seeger, Joan Baez (especially the first two recordings)

To listen to "The Rose and the Lindsy-O," "Buffalo Skinners," "Lord Bangam," and many other ballads mentioned in this text, see *In Yonder's Wood,* Willy and Brian Claflin (www.willyclaflin.com).

To ponder, in parting:

> *"If you ask a roomful of little kids, 'Who can sing?' everyone raises a hand. If you ask a roomful of adults, "Who can sing?" not a single hand goes up. What's that all about? Did they, like, forget?"*
>
> —BILL HARLEY

***WILLY CLAFLIN,** a full time performer and writer for the last 25 years, is a master storyteller, mostly for adults, but his kid fans are still really important. He is a favorite at the National Storytelling Festival and at regional festivals across the land. He tells original and traditional stories. Willy sings his own songs, plus 1,032 eerie ballads from the British Isles and Appalachia—and a lot of blues and rock and roll. He is also the speaking mouth person for Maynard Moose, another famous storyteller and kids' author. Learn more at www.willyclaflin.com.*

Storytelling Across Borders

LISTENING TO "THE OTHER"

Noa Baum

"An enemy is one whose story we have not heard."
MOTTO OF THE COMPASSIONATE LISTENING PROJECT

I grew up in Jerusalem, Israel. When my grandmother would hear the word Arab she would spit and say, "May their name be erased." Her son was killed in the war of 1948.

In 1993, when I lived in California, I met a woman on the playground. I knew she was a Palestinian, I recognized her beauty from home, but I didn't know if she'd want to talk to me. Nonetheless, I went up and asked her what her baby's name was and we started to talk. Over the years our kids grew up together and were friends. Then in 2000, I was working on creating a story based on my memories from the 1967 war when I was in third grade, and I realized that for the past seven years I had known this woman who grew up in Jerusalem, not five miles away from where I grew up, and I had never really heard what that war was like for her. I became curious and called her, and a very new chapter in our relationship began: we started to talk intensely. This time I asked questions, and for the first time in my life I heard what it actually felt like to be a Palestinian and live under Israeli occupation.

She told me that when she was ten, she saw a 14-year-old boy being beaten by soldiers and driven away. She said it was the first time she felt hate and understood what that word meant. For me, hearing this was like being hit in the gut. Those soldiers that she hated, that terrified and haunted her entire childhood, were my people, our boys, everyone that I knew that turned 18 and went to the army, including my brother! It was hard. But I kept listening because she was telling me her story.

We continued to talk. Eventually, we started to talk about our "history," the national narratives that are at the heart of the Israeli-Palestinian conflict. When I mentioned a known fact, what was the truth for me, she would say, "That's not true, that's Zionist propaganda!"

When she told me what was truth for her and what she learned at school as history, I would say, "That's not true at all, that's Arab propaganda!"

This would lead to arguing, but then she would say, "Look at us, we're getting defensive again." We would laugh and I would pick up the baby so that she could make a soft-boiled egg for the other kids. And we would continue to talk.

We were able to continue talking and listening to each other, in spite of the differences of not always agreeing, because we had trust and love between us, because we had heard each others' stories.

It was this very powerful experience that propelled me to create a performance piece based on our conversations called "A Land Twice Promised". In it I tell our personal stories that echo the contradictory national narratives of our people. I've been performing it internationally for the last eight years.

I realized that what I learned from this process could be useful for anyone dealing with issues of diversity:

- The way of listening deeply.
- The way stories allowed us to put aside our judgments and explore our differences in a non-threatening way.
- The fact that when we were telling each other our personal stories, it actually expanded our ability to accept things that were contradictory to everything we previously held as truth.

My story is not just about one woman connecting to another. It's not even about an Israeli connecting to a Palestinian. It's about the power of storytelling and the power of listening to the story of the "other," even and especially when that "other" is very different from you and when their story may be difficult to hear.

In workshops that I've developed for communities, interfaith groups, colleges and schools, participants are invited to share stories and learn to listen to "the other." Unlike sharing opinions and concepts, when we share a story we open up to another person's experience and something extraordinary happens.

First, Story shifts the emotional connection. In a very short time there's a sense of trust and intimacy. You may not know all the facts about that person, but you feel as if you have a glimpse into their world that is larger and deeper than you would have in other encounters.

> *"I can't believe how close I felt to someone after listening to a 3-minute story. I feel like I know this man and it's the first time in my life I actually got to sit and talk, heart to heart with an Islamic person and it did change my life."*
>
> —INTERFAITH WORKSHOP PARTICIPANT

It is not just the content of the story; it's the process of being in the same space, sharing your experience, listening and being listened to, that creates change.

Second, Story shifts the cognitive connection. We are attached to our thinking, our cognitive constructs of our world, our opinions. But when we listen to someone's story/experience we are using what Annette Simmons calls "the world's oldest form of virtual experience—the imagination." By using the imagination, we are able to look at the world in a way that is not ours and thus expand our ability to accept multiple/diverse points of view.

Being able to imagine and understand the point of view of "the other" does not mean you have to adopt it, or invalidate your older opinion. It just means you can virtually add another experience through your imagination.

Eventually adding on another's point of view may challenge your opinions or perhaps it may reveal misconceptions, but you don't have to change or replace it in the moment. It's not a declaration of defeat.

In a predominantly Mormon community, one of my workshop participants was listening to a story of someone who had an abortion. She said, *"For the first time in my life I was able to consider something that contradicted everything I believe in because I was listening to her story. I found myself being able to accept that abortion could be a valid option and even essential for someone else."*

Third, Story allows us to suspend judgment and expand our ability to hold multiple or contradicting points of view, or as Maxine Hong Kingston writes *"I tried to make my mind large, as the universe is large, so that there is room for paradoxes."* (*The Woman Warrior: Memoirs of Girlhood among Ghosts*, Vintage Books, 1975.) When I listened to my Palestinian friend's stories I was able to make my mind large, make room for paradox: hold a perception and interpretation that was different and foreign and even threatening to mine.

Simulating the technique I used in my performance piece, participants also learn to tell someone else's story from their point of view. The challenge of not only listening to someone else but *telling* the story of "the other" can deepen compassion and understanding for both the teller and listener.

Storytelling is a powerful tool to create trust, change attitudes, learn about other cultures and expand our ability to accept differences.

> *"This was really cool! I learned a lot about different religions and I became even more steadfast in my determination to change the world."*
>
> —TEENAGE PARTICIPANT, KANSAS CITY, KS

OBJECTIVES *for Grades Seven – Twelve*

(can be adjusted to Grades Four – Six)

Students will

- experience the power of individual stories to take us beyond rhetoric.
- develop understanding and tolerance of other cultures.
- explore connections to their culture.
- expand their ability to accept differences; enhance listening and communicating skills.
- deepen trust and build community.

INSTRUCTIONAL PLAN

I usually use my personal story as a modeling and springboard for the lesson plan. In situations where students have not heard the performance, I talk briefly about my personal experience that inspired the show and explain that in this lesson we will use a model I developed based on what I learned. I recommend sharing a personal experience as a point of entry to this lesson.

You may choose to tell:

- about a time in your life you met someone who was very different from you, or considered "the enemy."
- about a time you met someone who was always part of "them" and discovered you actually had a lot in common.

- about a time you formed an opinion about someone who was different without really knowing much about them, OR perhaps this happened to someone close to you, OR a time when you were judged or were "labeled."
- any personal experience that you can share about encountering "the other" will help engage the students and lead into the opening discussion.

Then lead a discussion with these questions:

- What are the things that make us who we are? (our traditions, families, nationalities, religion, gender)
- What do people fight about?
- Is there a way to claim who we are and let our difference move us closer to peace rather than to fighting? Let's try.

Finding a story

My instructions to the students go something like this:

1. Close your eyes and think of (choose one):
   - A special celebration in my family
   - A time I was grateful/proud to be part of my heritage/people/tradition
   - A time/event/person that made me feel I belonged to my heritage/people/tradition
2. Imagine the place where your story begins as if you're watching a movie in your mind's eye. See the details, what things look like. Who else is there?
3. Before sharing your story a few things to remember:
   - Share only what you are comfortable sharing, and that is okay for others to hear.
   - Listen to the story with no interruptions.
   - Listen to the story with delight: show attention with your eyes, face, and body.

Sharing the story

1. Students take turns sharing (90 seconds—2 minutes each)
2. After student A shared his/her story, give the following instruction: Before we switch: Listener, please give an appreciation (30 seconds).
   - What I liked about your story is __________.
   - A moment in your story that was especially vivid was __________.
3. Change roles: listeners now share their story and get an appreciation.
4. Reflect on the story you heard; turn to your partner and ask a curious question such as, "This ______ interests me. Can you say more about it?" or "I'm curious about ________. Could you tell me more?"
5. Partner answers. Change roles.

Reflection (with partner or as entire class)

1. How did it feel to tell?
2. How did it feel to listen and be listened to?

Deepening connections

1. With a new partner, tell your story again. Note: Is there anything that answering the "curious" question brought up for you that needs to be added or taken out of your story?
2. Listener gives an appreciation.
3. After each partner tells his or her story, close your eyes and see the story you heard as a movie in your mind.
4. Partners take turns asking each other questions. Get details about feelings, places, other people. Go beyond what things looked or sounded like—find out what they smelled, tasted, or felt like.

Putting yourself in someone else's shoes

1. With your partner, join another pair to form a group of four (or tell to the class)
2. Tell your partner's story using the first person ("I"). Make it sound like it happened to you.
3. A few things to keep in mind:
   - Do the best you can to stay true to the truth of the story.
   - NO imitation.
   - Don't worry about structure or plot. See if you can tell it as if it actually happened to you. Experiment with thoughts and feelings.

Group Feedback (each person gives appreciation)

1. What moments worked?
2. What did you like?

Discussion, reflection and questions

1. How did it feel to tell your story to someone?
2. How did it feel to hear your partner retell the story?
3. How did it feel to listen to someone else's story?
4. How did it feel to retell it?
5. How is storytelling different from debating or arguing?

Closing circle

Each student says, "One thing I'm taking away is _______."

ASSESSMENT

Ask students to identify and write about an issue of disagreement or dual perspectives that emerged from their storytelling experience, discussing the differences of viewpoint. Were there any shifts in personal viewpoints? If shifts occurred, explain why; if shifts did not occur, explain why not. Assess the writer's ability to articulate "the other's" point of view, and his/her degree of respect for that viewpoint.

NOA BAUM *is an award-winning Israeli storyteller and educator, focusing on her craft's power to heal across the divides of identity. Her show A Land Twice Promised relives her heartfelt dialogue with a Palestinian woman, illuminating the complex and contradictory history and emotions surrounding Jerusalem for Israelis and Palestinians alike. Noa performs and teaches internationally in hundreds of schools and organizations including The World Bank, U.S. Defense Dept., FDA, Kennedy Center, Mayo Clinic, and Brandeis University. Noa received an MA in Theater-in-Education from NYU, a Parents' Choice Recommended Award and multiple Individual Artist Awards from Maryland State Arts Council and AHCMC. More information: www.noabaum.com*

Is It Deep Enough?

WHAT DO AFRICAN AND AFRICAN-AMERICAN FOLKTALES TELL US ABOUT THE PEOPLE WHO GAVE THEM LIFE?

Charlotte Blake Alston

"How Sandy Got His Meat" is an African-American trickster tale. In the story, a pond-full of frogs get wise to a frog-snatching raccoon named Sandy and decide to stay below the water whenever they see him coming. Fox devises a plan that will get Sandy all the frog meat he desires. He convinces Sandy to play dead and accuses the frogs of contributing to his demise by starving him to death. Since they are responsible for his death, Fox tells them, they should also take responsibility for burying him. The frogs dig around and under Sandy so his body sinks lower as the earth around him is dug away. After some time, they look up and ask Fox, "Is it deep enough?" "Can you jump out?" Fox asks. The frogs jump, leaping effortlessly out of the hole. "Nope, not yet," they croak in unison. They continue digging around and under Sandy for a while and ask again, "Is it deep enough?" "Can you jump out?" comes Fox's reply. This time they jump high enough to just make it out of the hole. Again, they croak, "Nope, not yet!" They continue digging then ask, "Is it deep enough?" "Can you jump out?" They try leaping as high as they can, but finally, not one is able to escape the hole. Fox leans over and says, "Rise up Sandy and get your meat!" Sandy opens his eyes and all around him are fat, juicy frogs.

Much of our information about the rich, diverse continent of Africa comes from nature programs or the evening news. Many of those stories begin with the reporter saying, "In Africa today..." The continent is referred to and spoken of as though it were a country. "In Africa today..." is a lead-in that usually offers us a story about something happening in one village, town, city, or region of one country. The language leads the viewer to believe that this event, concentrated in one specific location, is taking place throughout the entire continent. The cumulative effect of these stories constitutes a misrepresentation of the continent's diversity and a dismissal of its 54 independent nations, instead presenting the continent and its diverse regions, countries and peoples as a monolith.

The misinformation, age-old stereotypes, and misrepresentation persist in today's news coverage and in the language of the copy writer often coupled with the reporter's own Western-influenced perceptions. A journalist reporting from a small village in Kenya started with, "In Africa everyone says *jambo.*" That's like saying, "In Europe, everyone says *guten tag.*" People who speak the Kiswahili language say *'jambo.'* People who live elsewhere and speak one of the hundreds of other languages do not. In yet another example, a reporter on his first trip to the continent, covering a presidential visit, spoke of how "scary" and "mysterious" it felt. It turned out that he was reporting from downtown Dakar, outside the 48-track recording studio of world music icon, Youssou Ndour, whom the reporter was about to interview! I'm still trying to figure out what was so scary about a 48-track recording studio. So even though we, the viewers, were seeing the reporter's actual surroundings—a busy city thoroughfare with lots of foot traffic—he was essentially telling us to believe that what we were seeing was not really what we were seeing, but that his 'African' surroundings were actually mysterious and frightful. Really?

We all internalize this language of misperception. As I stood awaiting some traveling companions in the lobby of a hotel in Accra, Ghana, a gentleman started up a conversation. It was his second day in Accra and he expressed to me his disappointment that he had not yet seen any animals or big game. I gently offered that it was highly unlikely that he was going to encounter elephants waiting for a restaurant table or hyenas in line at the bank in downtown Accra. He would have to venture a tad further out or catch a flight across the continent to a game preserve in Uganda, Kenya, Tanzania or South Africa. Okay, yes, I was a tad facetious.

I was a young woman in the 1960s when I first encountered African folktales. As I dug deeper, I reached a new depth where I found knowledge and received nourishment from the sweet meat of my own rich ancestry and cultural traditions.

Now, whenever I find an African folktale I wish to tell, I begin researching its ethnic origins. If possible, I identify and make contact with someone from that ethnic group or geographic region. Those conversations reveal layers of meaning sometimes missing from the translated versions and subsequent variations of the source story.

Once, at the end of a storytelling performance, a woman approached me and asked if one story I told wasn't in fact a story about Satan. A python figures prominently in the story. Based on her own belief system, a snake could only be a symbol of evil, nothing else. In fact, some of the most poisonous snakes on planet Earth—including the black mamba—reside in the land of the Shona people of Zimbabwe where the story originates. People must be knowledgeable about the habits of each in order to avoid tragic, even deadly, encounters. It was discovered long ago that parts of the python could be used in making medicines. So snakes have been incorporated into the folklore of the people, since they are such a prominent feature in the landscape. A friend, South African musician, artist, sculptor, and storyteller Mahowane Mahloele told me, "You don't even know a black mamba is anywhere near you until it is looking you in the eye—and then it is too late! Zulu warriors studied the ways of the black mamba. If you could move as a black mamba moved, strike as a black mamba struck, you were considered a fearsome warrior indeed."

In the land of the indigenous Khoi-San people of South Africa, you will find an abundance of praying mantises. As a result, the folklore of the San includes many stories of Mantis—also called Kaggen.

As with many ancient tales, African and African-American stories often offer information about the location, time, historical context, and life circumstances of their creators. During the period of enslavement in America, African Americans were not considered human and were therefore spoken to and spoken about in demeaning, dehumanizing terms. For years after emancipation, on through the civil rights struggle of the 1950s and '60s, much of the essence of the hard work and struggle was about dignity and respect. Adult men and women were still addressed by white Americans as 'Boy' or 'Girl.' They, in turn, were expected to use the word 'Sir' or Ma'am' when addressing a white person.

In a wonderful independent school where I once taught, an absence of knowledge, understanding, and an appreciation of both this history as well as an age-old standard African and African-American ethical sensibility eventually became an issue. In the spirit of manifesting a belief in the equality of all, children addressed adults by their first names—but with the honorific 'Teacher' when addressing faculty members. 20+ years later, I am still referred to as 'Teacher Charlotte' by former students now in their 30s. Among the faculty of 70, only three were persons of color. Two African-American women on the administrative staff insisted on being addressed with the title 'Mrs.' The problem arose with regard to the cafeteria and maintenance staff, all of whom were African American. Certainly, the intent was not to be demeaning, but without any knowledge of or understanding of African or African-American history, or cultural sensibilities, Black adults were being addressed by predominantly white school-age children—preK-12th grade—by their first names only, as though they were the children's peers. Generally among African Americans, this is the height of disrespect. Even in a time when civility has diminished in American culture and profanity and vulgarity seem to be embraced as normal, children in African-American communities do not address adults by their first names unless that adult has given them permission to do so. Adults are addressed as Mr. or Mrs./Miss Jones. If you use an adult's first name, the title Mr. or Miss nearly always precedes it: i.e., Miss Gerri or Mr. Bob.

This is still standard in many African cultures today. Remnants of social mores such as this one followed Africans to American shores, where even under conditions of enslavement, building a sense of family and community and maintaining respect for one another in the midst of hardship remained important. The use of the titles 'Sister,' 'Brother,' 'Uncle,' or 'Aunt' to address older non-relatives was common.

Enter Br'er Rabbit. Enter Sis' Possum, Br'er Bear, Br'er Fox and Sis' Alligator. The central body of African-American folktales emerged during the period of enslavement. Thoughts, feelings, emotions, opinions that could not be expressed directly to a plantation owner, sharecropper foreman, or later, a demeaning or unfair employer, got expressed in the tales. People's tongues could be 'loosened' through Br'er Rabbit. Br'er Rabbit always manages—in the end—to outwit, outsmart or trick a larger more physically powerful animal. He is a survivor. He always manages to ESCAPE and to remain FREE to live another day.

A prominent figure in African-American folklore we don't hear about as much as Br'er Rabbit is High John the Conqueror (sometimes pronounced 'conker' or 'conqueroo'). High John possessed super human powers that he would harness to gain the upper hand on slave masters or to even 'fly above' his circumstances. But High John often lifted others as well. At other times, he outwitted the plantation owner with a riddle or trick.

Let's take a look at or revisit a few folktales and see what they might reveal or teach about their creators. Let's dig just a little bit deeper to access the meat of African and African American oral and cultural tradition. It is my hope that the following activities will stimulate your own interest and ideas for creating activities that take you and your students a little bit deeper.

OVERALL OBJECTIVES

Students will

- be exposed to and immersed in African and African-American folktales.
- enhance research skills.
- enhance expressive language.
- be encouraged in oral expression and self-confidence in speaking in front of a group.
- be able to speak confidently from a base of knowledge.
- be introduced to the diversity of the African continent, its countries, ethnic groups, peoples and languages.
- learn the names of African countries, ethnic groups, and languages.
- learn and use words for 'hello' and 'thank you' in diverse African languages.
- learn, analyze and discuss proverbs from the African continent.
- research, read and listen to a variety of stories from the African and African-American folklore traditions.
- learn and tell one story from the African and one from the African-American tradition.
- learn and make immediate use of new vocabulary.
- make connections between the folktales and the people who created them.
- practice listening, observing analyzing, questioning and the stories and information they receive from media sources, books and their own one-on-one or group conversations about other people and cultures.
- become competent storytellers.
- have fun!!

INSTRUCTIONAL PLANS

Preliminary Unit: Africa: Setting the Stage

(Optional but strongly encouraged)

PART 1: WHAT WE KNOW: LAYING A FOUNDATION

MATERIALS

- chart paper
- marker

STEP 1 In capital letters, write the word AFRICA at the top of a sheet of chart paper.

STEP 2 Ask students what comes to mind when they hear the word. What do they already know?

STEP 3 Write student responses on the chart paper. Use more if necessary.

STEP 4 Teacher's choice: Option 1—leave the list in plain sight. Option 2—set the list aside. You will return to it later.

PART 2: AFRICA IS NOT A COUNTRY

MATERIALS

- black and white copy of a map of the African continent with countries clearly identified for each student
- large world map or large classroom map of the African continent.

STEP 1 To get a sense of the diversity of the African continent, working in pairs or small groups, have students research the names of African countries. Each student should identify and write down the name of at least five countries, then read the names aloud to each other.

STEP 2 Have students research and identify the names of ethnic groups (between 3 and 5) residing in the countries they have chosen. Each student should list the names, then take turns speaking each one aloud to each other.

STEP 3 Hand out student copies of the maps. Each student should identify and color in the countries they have chosen. Teacher's choice: you can have students color code the map by designating a color for each part of the continent; for example, yellow for countries in the north, green for the west, orange for Central Africa, etc.

STEP 4 Display a classroom map of the continent. Ask students to name a country from their list. Ask each student who volunteers to step forward and identify the country on the classroom map. Others who identified the same country should raise their hands. Select a student to mark the country with a push-pin or a small representative flag. You can find images of each country's flag online.

STEP 5 Number and list all countries identified on chart paper. Leave in a visible place.

PART 3: 'AFRICAN' IS NOT A LANGUAGE

While multiple languages are spoken in all African countries, some European languages—English, French, or Portuguese—are listed as 'official' languages in many of them. These languages were imposed onto people during European colonization. Encourage your students to learn words from indigenous languages.

STEP 1 Have students research and identify the names of languages spoken in the countries they have chosen.

STEP 2 Have students research and identify the word from each language that means 'hello.'

STEP 3 Repeat the same for the phrase 'thank you.'

STEP 4 From the students' research, make a master list with five columns on chart paper. List all the countries, corresponding ethnic groups, languages, and corresponding words they have found. See sample chart. In some instances, the ethnic group name and language name are the same: the Wolof of Senegal speaks Wolof.

COUNTRY	ETHNIC GROUP	LANGUAGE	HELLO/HOW ARE YOU?	THANK YOU
Malawi	Chiwa	Chechewa	Moni	Zikomo

STEP 5 Students should share their lists aloud within their group or have all students stand and partner with a classmate. On the teacher's instruction and signal, each student shares their list. Allow one minute per student, then signal them to switch (two minutes per pairing). Upon the teacher's signal, each student moves and pairs with a different classmate. Continue until students have had three or four opportunities to share. Select a few students to share their list with the class.

STEP 6 Ask students to choose a different language from their list each day and use those words for 'hello' and 'thank you' throughout the day—even when they are greeting other students or adults in the school building!

PART 4: AFRICAN PROVERBS

MATERIALS

- list of African proverbs
- sentence strips (I use the multi-colored strips)
- thick black marker.

In the form of a simple phrase, proverbs embody and express profound wisdom, universal truths from accumulated knowledge gained and passed down through the ages. A proverb or two is often stated at the beginning, but more often at the end of the teller's tale. They are infused in conversations and debates and referred to in the midst of difficult circumstances. Many hold a general belief that today's problems can be resolved by examining the wisdom and lessons of the past.

TEACHER PREPARATION

- Assemble a list of African proverbs from books. There are several collections. You can also Google: African proverbs

STEP 1 Write half of each selected proverb on one sentence strip, the second half on another. On the back lower corner of the strip, write the name of the proverb's country of origin or ethnic group with a pen. Generally, I give four students the same proverb; two have one half, two have the other. You can revise that to make the discussion groups larger or to do it in pairs only.

STEP 2 Introduce the word 'proverb' and its definition. Inform students that proverbs are and have historically been an integral part of African storytelling and social interaction.

STEP 3 Tell students that they will each receive one half of a proverb. Their job is to find the classmate with the other half. They will do this by approaching a classmate and reading their proverb portion, then listening to the classmate's half. Students should determine if the two halves make sense and form a whole. If so, they look for the two additional classmates who have the same proverb. Allot approximately 10-15 minutes. You may be surprised at how quickly they find each other.

STEP 4 Students should now sit in their 'proverb groups' and discuss the meaning of the proverb and if it is applicable to them or today's modern society in any way. They should also consider if they've heard a similar proverb or saying from any other culture or time. They should also look on the back to find their proverb's origin.

STEP 5 Each 'proverb group' then shares with the class both their proverb and their understanding of its meaning and its potential application in today's world.

STEP 6 After each proverb is shared, pose the following questions: Do you think the proverb says anything about the people who live by it? Explain. Does the proverb help you understand anything you may not have understood before? Explain.

Unit 1: Inside African Folktales— Learning, Listening, and Telling

MATERIALS

- Written copies and/or audio recordings of a variety of African folktales. Your community or school librarian is a great resource for this! Stock your classroom with them.

TEACHER PREPARATION

- Include stories of Anansi, Sungura, or Hlakayana, the signature trickster characters from Ghana, Kenya and the Zulu of South Africa, respectively. Include "Why Stories" and dilemma tales.
- The recounting and preservation of history was the primary role of the West African griot, but many of the historical epics can take hours or days to recount. The most child-friendly account of Sundiata Keita, the great Lion King of Mali, (yes, he was a person) is a well done English translation and retelling by David Wisniewski with beautiful cut-paper illustrations. To deepen your own understanding you may consider reading a more detailed version by D.T. Niane to get a better historical perspective on this revered history.

STEP 1 Set aside a time each day to read a folktale aloud to your class or tell a folktale you have learned. It's important that they hear stories. Have fun playing with the inflections and nuances of your voice.

STEP 2 Let the folktale exploration begin! Allow students to spend several days or sessions reading a variety of tales. Then each student should select one to learn.

STEP 3 Divide students into story groups or villages. Let them come up with a folktale character-based name; i.e., "The Anansi Story Group" or "The Sundiata Story Village." Students should first practice their chosen story with a partner. Then in story groups, allow students to take turns telling their chosen story to the group. Repeat this part of the step for several days.

STEP 4 Refer to "Questions for Discussion" below. In pairs or in small groups ask students to consider, discuss and write down their responses to the questions.

STEP 5 Follow with a class discussion of the questions.

STEP 6 Go Forth and Tell! Allow each student an opportunity to tell his/her chosen story to the entire class. Discuss and create opportunities for telling the stories the students have learned outside of the classroom: visits in pairs to other classes, administrative offices, an assembly presentation, or even off-school sites such as senior centers. Consider inviting parents in for a Storytelling Day.

STEP 7 Extend an invitation to someone from an African country who may reside in the community, be in attendance or teaching at a local college or university to come and share with your class. In exchange, invite several students to share with the guest the stories they have learned.

STEP 8 Finally, return to your 'Africa: what we know' list. Ask your students what on the list they would now add, eliminate, or change. What are they aware of now that they were not aware of before? Has anything changed about what you knew or thought or what you didn't know? Explain.

Unit 2: Inside African-American Folktales—Learning, Listening, and Telling

MATERIALS:

- Written copies and/or audio recordings of a variety of African American folktales and songs. Your community or school librarian is a great resource for this! Stock your classroom with them. Often, songs are treasured as much as stories. Consider including and play recordings of call-and-response songs and games of Bessie Jones or the Georgia Sea Island Singers.

TEACHER PREPARATION

- Include stories of Br'er Rabbit, High John the Conqueror, and 'Freedom' stories.
- Follow steps 1 through 5 in Unit 1

ASSESSMENT

Questions for discussion: write some or all of them for students to consider.

- Are you able to determine what African country or ethnic group gave birth to your story?
- Can you find the story's birthplace on a map? What languages are spoken there?
- What does the story reveal about the place where it was created?
- What does the story tell you about what types of animals can be found there?
- What does the story reveal about the time it was created?
- What do the stories reveal about how observant the storytellers were about local plant and animal life?
- What characteristics does the central character display? Courage? Deceit? Stamina? Persistence? Perseverance? Wisdom? Self-confidence? Thoughtlessness? Impatience? Intelligence? Ability to solve problems? Survival Instincts? Ability to predict an outcome?
- How observant is he? Does he demonstrate knowledge about other animals' personalities, habits and behavior?
- Does that knowledge—or lack thereof—serve the character in any way?
- What is the relationship between the animal characters?
- What is the relationship between the human characters in the story?
- When the characters are both animals and people, what is the relationship between them?
- What does the story tell you about the kinds of food people may have eaten?
- What does the story tell you about the kind of work people did?
- Do you have any thoughts about why this kind of story would be important and popular among the people who created it?

- Unique among African-American folktales is the way animals are addressed and how the animals greet each other as Br'er or Sis' even where they are wary or suspicious of each other. First, each of those titles is an abbreviated form of what words? Second, do you have any thoughts or ideas about why the characters are referred to in that way? Why would this be important to the stories' creators?
- Do you find any similarities between the African folktales you have read, heard and told, and the African-American tales?

RESOURCES

Consult with your school, community and university libraries and librarians, and surf the internet—you can type in a subject, story genre, character name, etc. and access any number of resources.

Suggested Stories

(Feel free to incorporate other wonderful stories in these collections.)

- "Mantis and the Moon." Mandela, Nelson. *Nelson Mandela's Favorite Folktales.* NY: W.W. Norton & Company, 2002 (American Publisher); Cape Town, South Africa: Tafelburg Publishers Ltd., 2002 (South African publisher).
- "Nanabolele, Who Shines in the Night." Postma, Minnie. *Tales from the Basotho.* American Folklore Society Memoir Series, Vol. 59. Austin, TX: University of Texas Press, 1974.
- A version of "Nanabolele" can also be found in Kathleen Ragan's *Wise Girls, Fearless Women and Beloved Sisters.* (Norton & Company, 1998). A recorded version of "Nanabolele" can be found on the compact disc *What Little Girls Are Made Of* (Charlotte Blake Alston, www.charlotteblakealston.com)
- "Nonikwe and the Great One, Marimba." Mutwa, Credo Vusa'mazulu. *Indaba My Children.* London: Kahn and Averill, Stanmore Press Ltd., 1966.
- A version of "Nonikwe" can also be found in Kathleen Ragan's *Fearless Girls, Wise Women and Beloved Sisters.* (W.W. Norton & Company, 1998), pp. 354-358; a recorded version of "Nonikwe" can be found on the compact disc *What Little Girls Are Made Of* (Charlotte Blake Alston, www.charlotteblakealston.com)

- "The Lion's Whiskers." Ashbrenner, Brent and Russell Davis. *The Lion's Whiskers and Other Ethiopian Tales.* Hamden, CT: Linnet Books, 1997
- "The People Could Fly." Hamilton, Virginia. *The People Could Fly: American Black Folktales.* NY: Alfred A. Knopf, 1985.
- "The River that Went to the Sky: A Story From Malawi." Mendicott, Mary and Ademola Akintola. *The River That Went to the Sky: 12 Tales by African Storytellers.* NY: Kingfisher, 1985.

Also recommended

- Appiah, Peggy. *Tales of an Ashanti Father.* Boston: Beacon Press, 1967. You will find Anansi stories and other Ashanti tales.
- Kantor, Susan, ed. *One Hundred and One African American Read Aloud Stories.* NY: Black Dog and Leventhal Publishers, 1998. This is a collection of both African and African American folktales, historical stories, proverbs, songs, chants and more.
- Niane, D.T. *Sundiata: an Epic of Old Mali.* Essex, England: Longman-Pearson Education Limited, 1965. Original French version: Présence Africaine, 1960.
- Wisniewski, David. *Sundiata: Lion King of Mali.* NY: Clarion Books, 1992. This is a beautifully illustrated condensed retelling of the epic story of the boy who overcame enormous obstacles to become the great ruler of the Mali empire in the 13th century. When the story is retold by the griots, it is done with drumming, music, dancing and singing. It can take one or more days for the epic to be retold.

***CHARLOTTE BLAKE ALSTON** is a nationally acclaimed storyteller, narrator, instrumentalist, singer and concert host who performs in educational and concert venues throughout North America and abroad. She serves as guest host and narrator on both family and school concerts for The Philadelphia Orchestra (since 1991) and Carnegie Hall (since 1995). She has received numerous honors and awards including a Pew Fellowship in the Arts, the Commonwealth of PA. Artist of the Year Award, the National Storytelling Network's Circle of Excellence Award and the Zora Neale Hurston Award, the highest award conferred by the National Association of Black Storytellers. Learn more about Charlotte Blake Alston at www.charlotteblakealston.com*

Indians Shop at Wal-Mart

Tim Tingle

First, some amazingly good news! On June 14, 2011, a group of American Indian library advocates, led by Choctaw Susan Feller and Comanche Lotsee Patterson, met in Washington, D.C. with John Cole, Director of the American Center for the Book. As a result, the Library of Congress approved the formation of the American Indian Center for the Book (AICB).

Within a few short years, this landmark government recognition will be felt in every community in America large enough to have a library. Plans are already underway for Indian-produced digital magazines, ebooks, downloadable posters for use on grade school campuses, curriculum guides, with a blog and website; in short, a place to go for the rapidly growing and now-numbering-in-the-thousands of educators who strive to inform students with insightful and powerful truths about American Indians.

The first book sponsored by the AICB, which I have been asked to edit, will be a collection of traditional and contemporary stories written by some of our country's most renowned Native authors and storytellers, including Joe Bruchac and N. Scott Momaday. A national tour of American Indian storytellers will promote the book and give the AICB national exposure. American Indians can now step away from their computers for a moment, take the elevator to the ground floor, step out on the sidewalk, and lift praises to the sky!

"Did you really think you could
destroy our medicine with freeways?"
CHOCTAW POET, ROXY GORDON

As you read this article I want you, the reader, to catch a glimpse of the intensity of my hope. In a workshop at the Smithsonian in Washington, D.C., the director of the National Museum of the American Indian, Dr. Kevin Gover, said, "People come to our museum with all varieties of misconceptions about Indians. We need to meet people on the bridge they cross." Many Americans want to know more about Native Americans, and rather than focus on what they do not know, we must lead them respectfully on a trip to a better-informed knowledge base.

So, please allow me to be your guide, *Hattak Kana* (Friendly Man in Choctaw). Following some observations, I will suggest possible classroom activities.

American history tends to start with the landing of Columbus, and, rather than struggling with that endless argument, in the spirit of *Hattak Kana,* let's go along with it. Why? Because an obsession with how Native People lived in pre-Columbian times takes us to that precarious edge, the strongly implanted belief that Indians are primitive people.

In 1492, most American Indians (or Native Americans, whichever you prefer) lived in permanent homes made of wood. They lived in towns of sometimes tens of thousands of people. They enjoyed the benefits of local, state, and national governments. Towns usually included schools for the young and churches for worshipping. Unfortunately, in America as well as Europe, most citizens could not read. But with the introduction of books by friendly Europeans as early as the 1790s, many schools adapted and soon included reading and writing as part of daily instruction.

Now, let us look at the buffalo culture, one we all know:

In the late 1870s, at the height of this culture, less than five percent of Indians depended on the buffalo. For the overwhelming majority of Indians of that time, the word 'buffalo,' in their native language, referred to a now-extinct animal that dashed in and out of pine trees on the eastern seaboard, and in Mississippi, Alabama, and the Carolinas. This buffalo was about the size of a deer and quick as lightning. By the early 1800s, many Indian war veterans, having served in the United States Army in the War of 1812, would rise early, say goodbye to their families, and slip into the nearby woods with their shotguns for "buffalo hunting," as deer hunters do today.

By the beginning of the twentieth century, Indians as a general rule dressed in woven cloth, much as Chickasaw Indian John Herrington wears to work, before donning his NASA suit for a trip to the space shuttle. Indian attorneys, movie actors, and politicians, as well as Indian electricians, often wear clothing made of woven cloth today; though the clothing is not woven on Navajo looms, but rather stitched together overseas and can be purchased by non-Indians and Indians alike at popular department stores and outlet malls. Even Wal-Mart!

Hoke! (Okay in Choctaw)...Friendly Man is trying to make his point with humor... The point can be summarized easily. We Indians are proud of our heritage, and would much prefer that the study of Indian culture and history be ongoing and include modern Indian heroes from every walk of life.

JOHN HERRINGTON

LOUISE ERDICH

SAM BRADFORD

In a few weeks I will resume working and commence traveling in Hawaii, Minnesota, Oklahoma, and Texas. That's September. I travel in two worlds. World One is a world of public and private schools, universities, literary and storytelling festivals. World Two is Indian, as I am. I attend Indian research conferences, Choctaw gatherings, and perform at Native American events, most recently Choctaw Days at the Smithsonian.

The differences are stark. Within the circle of my friends, World Two, Indians are winning Fulbright scholarships, delivering keynote addresses, and serving on key committees in the United States Congress. Dr. Lorriene Roy, an Anishinabe enrolled on the White Earth Reservation, served in 2007-2008 as President of the American Library Association.

TOM COLE

DR. LORRIENE ROY

JIM THORPE

ACTOR ADAM BEACH WITH ICE-T

LOTSEE PATTERSON

In contrast, World One celebrates Native American Month in November. Bulletin boards on many school campuses display Indians wearing headdresses, riding ponies, and chasing buffaloes. If anyone on the bulletin board has a name, it is Pocahontas, Sacajawea, or, if educators chose to display a modern Indian, Jim Thorpe. We love and respect Jim Thorpe, but he would roll from his grave, football helmet in hand, if he knew the current state of Indian studies in schools today.

Do we need a new approach to Native American history?

No.

We need a new approach to American history, for the two Worlds are inseparable.

Two evenings ago I watched *She Wore a Yellow Ribbon*, a film starring John Wayne. The villains were Indians, wearing feathers and firing bows and arrows. They spoke in broken English and evoked unthinkable cruelties on settlers. A closing scene depicts a Cheyenne elder urging John Wayne to join him on a buffalo hunt. "We can smoke pipes and drink whiskey!" says the elder. For two decades an entire generation of Americans saw these and similar movies, starring America's most popular star of the time, John Wayne.

Why is this important? Consider this: Just as I was subjected to a barrage of fascinating and unforgettable visual images from Hollywood, educational decision-makers of my generation watched them, too.

Famed actor Adam Beach, when asked about his critically-acclaimed portrayal of Ira Hayes in the Clint Eastwood film, *Flags of Our Fathers*, replied, "For me, it was an ultimate achievement. Look at the history of Native American people in Hollywood: they have not been represented in a human way on film. Hollywood has portrayed such a negative image of who we are as people."

Book-buyers, librarians or the general public, continue to purchase books reflecting these negative images. Teachers who want to be culturally sensitive, or just want to tell the truth, have no materials, and the library has few answers. Even today, the larger publishing community prefers books promoting these untruths.

Why?

Because they sell.

Why?

Because they give the reader what the reader wants: feathers and animal skins.

Why?

Because strongly planted visual images from half a century ago take precedence over discussions and lectures.

What is the answer?

Time. The answer is time and a life-long commitment from a growing and determined few, Indians and non-Natives.

After twenty years of speaking on school campuses in the United States and abroad, I have come to realize that what we are teaching our youngest students is more in line with 60-year-old films than the reality of Indian life. In the fall of 2010, I spoke to a group of fourth graders who had just completed their Native American history unit. I spoke of tribal governments, of current issues over water rights.

A student raised his hand and said, "Why are you telling us this? Indians are dead."

I hope someday in the future that intelligent young man will read this article, because I was too dumbstruck at the time to give him a good answer.

What I should have said: "No, son, Indians are not dead. Only in your classroom and on your bookshelves are they dead. Indians are alive and thriving and contributing to our American way of life. You cannot realize this because, even though you see dozens and sometimes hundreds of Indians every week, you never recognize them."

Why?

You do not recognize them because they are not dressed like the Indians of your history unit.

If you've made it this far, and are willing to forgive *Hattak Kana* for removing his headdress, here are some classroom activities:

Let's begin with a storytelling exercise. Since we are striving to identify and rethink stereotypes, we'll try modern stories first, folktales later. Years later, for we must replace those damaging visual images with pictures like 1.8 and 1.9, of an actor and a librarian:

- For non-Native students, consider telling an Indian removal story, told in the voice of a young person. For an example, see "Trail of Tears," from my first book, *Walking the Choctaw Road* (Cintos Puntos, 2003).
- For all students, a short biographical story of a modern American Indian hero would be a great place to start.

For teachers:

- Define and discuss stereotypes. Who do they hurt? Identify some commonly believed Indian stereotypes.
- For middle and high school students, ask the rarely considered question: Who benefits from stereotypes? Who do they help?
- Why do we cling to these false images of Native Americans?
- Consider showing the best American Indian stereotype demolition film of all time, *Reel Injun*. Written and directed by Cree tribal member Neil Diamond, the film examines Hollywood's depiction of American Indians from silent to contemporary films. Included are interviews with Native and non-Native actors, critics, celebrities, and historians. The film is insightful and a joy to watch. Scenes that most Americans find acceptable and accurate suddenly appear not only racist, but ludicrous.
- By use of photos from the internet, have students create a bulletin board, including brief biographies, of modern American Indians, heroes and everyday people. Here are some names to research: John Herrington, Leslie Marmon Silko, N. Scott Momaday, Walter Echo-Hawk, Lorriene Roy, Sam Bradford, Joe Bruchac, Billy Mills, James Earl Jones, Ben Nighthorse Campbell, Greg Pyle. For additional help, my Choctaw friend Greg Rodgers and I have created a website, and you can download bulletin board-ready photos and brief bios: NativeAmBB.com

- Have students take a field trip to the school library. Locate all books related to American Indians. Compare those written by Indians with those written by non-Native American authors. What are some differences? (note in particular tribal identification. For example, is the book marketed as "an Indian folktale," or a Cherokee traditional story?) Which books accurately depict American Indians and which would be more likely to re-enforce stereotypes?
- Assign a panel discussion of the best-selling Indian book of all time: *The Education of Little Tree* (Carter, Forrest. Delacourte Press, 1976). Be sure to include the insightful articles from Debbie Reese's blog site: http://americanindiansinchildrensliterature.blogspot.com/
- Have students compare earlier reviews of the book to the article written by Dan T. Carter, a family member of the author's, in the *New York Times,* October 4, 1991. Be sure to share this insightful article with other faculty members.
- Launch a school-wide search; Find the Indians! Every campus has unrecognized (by students) Native Americans. Ask Indian faculty, staff, and students to speak briefly about their tribe, and how they learned about their heritage. If they know little, learn together. Tribal websites are a great place to start. I'll be glad to assist with "where do I find info on this Indian nation?" questions. (Especially if you refer to nations rather than tribes).

☆☆☆☆☆ FIVE STAR IDEA!

For a writing assignment, have students research an American Indian nation's history. Write a short video game narrative, with dialogue, heroes, and villains. A great reference source is *Bury My Heart at Wounded Knee,* Dee Brown's classic (Holt, Rinehart & Winston, 1970). Maybe Andrew Jackson could be a villain, for his actions on the Trail of Tears, or maybe the soldiers at Wounded Knee or Sand Creek. Try alternate endings, with super-powered cool Indians creating a universe where the waters do flow freely. For everybody: Arrange the best gamers in class in small groups, after they have done their research, to discuss character and plot ideas.

"Hoke," Hattak Kana is taking a deep breath before writing words he has never written, sharing happenings that should be known. Are you ready?

- My own great-great grandmother died of smallpox from blankets passed out by government employees—with full knowledge of what they were doing.
- As late as the 1970s, our homes were destroyed and flooded—in our lifetimes—from Seneca Nation in upstate New York to Yosemite Park in California.
- Only two decades ago, homes sitting atop a beautiful and remote mesa in Laguna Country, New Mexico, were shaken to the foundation by illegal uranium mining nearby, and several Laguna residents contacted cancer and died.

Why do stereotypes hurt? In 1879, the United States District Court in Omaha, Nebraska, (case of Standing Bear *versus* Crook) declared that Indians are, in fact, human. But movie Indians seldom acted as civilized Americans. Maybe the perpetrators of the aforementioned crimes believed the movie versions, the bulletin board versions. Please help us to eradicate these images and replace them with a healthier truth. I encourage you to read the essay to my most recent children's book, *Saltypie* (Cintos Puntos, 2010).

Let us close with a quote from Standing Bear, spoken at his trial. *"(My) hand is not the color of yours, but if I prick it, the blood will flow, and I shall feel pain. The blood is of the same color as yours. God made me, and I am a man."*

What we want more than anything is respect. We are strong people or we would never have survived. But we did survive, and we'd like for you to join us in celebrating the updated, 21st century American Indian! It's a good day to live!

Bless your efforts!
Hattak Kana, Tim Tingle.

TIM TINGLE is an Oklahoma Choctaw and an award-winning author. ***Crossing Bok Chitto****, Tingle's first illustrated book, won over twenty state and national awards, inspired two award-winning plays, and was an editor's Choice Book by the New York Times. His most recent children's book,* ***Saltypie****, was selected as an American Library Association Notable Book for 2011. He has performed at the Smithsonian, the Kennedy Center, the Library of Congress, and as a featured storyteller in forty-four states and Canada, sharing traditional and personal American Indian stories while playing the cedar flute and whaleskin drum. www.timtingle.com*

Another sankofa, used as both sculptured image
and pictograph, is that of a mythical bird, flying forward
with its head turned backward, and with an egg
in its mouth or with the egg being taken from its back.
This symbol both reflects the concept of sankofa,
the Akan belief that the past serves as a guide for the
present and future, that the wisdom in remembering
and learning from the past is essential to personal
development and growth.

CHAPTER TWO

National Council of Social Studies 2. Time, Continuity & Change

Social studies programs should include experiences that provide for the study of the past and its legacy.

Studying the past makes it possible for us to understand the human story across time.

Knowledge and understanding of the past enable us to analyze the causes and consequences of events and developments, and to place these in the context of the institutions, values, beliefs of the periods in which they took place.

Knowing how to read, reconstruct and interpret the past allows us to answer questions such as How do we learn about the past? How can we evaluate the usefulness and degree of reliability of different historical sources? What are the roots of our social, political and economic systems? What are our personal roots and how can they be viewed as part of human history? Why is the past important to us today? How has the world changed and how might it change in future? How do perspectives about the past differ, and to what extent do these differences inform contemporary ideas and actions?

Children in early grades learn to locate themselves in time and space.

Through a more formal study of history, students in the middle grades continue to expand their understanding of the past and are increasingly able to apply the research methods associated with historical inquiry.

LYN FORD | KATE ANDERSON | BETH HORNER
ADRIENNE & SYD LIEBERMAN | SHERRY NORFOLK
ALTON CHUNG | DONNA WASHINGTON
MEGAN GERAGHTY & KATIE ALLEN & KRISTIN PILLIOD
JO RADNER

Sankofa

GO BACK AND GET IT

Lyn Ford

You may have noticed the adinkra images and their associated proverbs above the Foreword, the Introduction, the Table of Contents and above each chapter. An adinkra image is both sculptured image and pictograph, ideographic reminders of the importance of wisdom and heritage. As early as the 1400s, the metalwork, woodcarving, textile creations, and ceramics of the Akan people of West Africa were recognized for their intricate beauty. Metal art in castings of gold, iron, and brass were of value as treasures of the British colony then known as the Gold Coast (1821-1957). The work of Ghanaian craftsmen is still displayed as fine sculpture and creative art. It deserves this recognition, though the work was never meant to be art created merely for art's sake.

Each work's development and construction is a part of traditions of familial and cultural knowledge, apprenticeship, and narrative skill offered through visual imagery, story, and proverb. The abstract meanings of fables and proverbs become subtle and sophisticated, yet concrete gems of wisdom that can be seen, touched, held, absorbed, and routinely experienced in the living of one's day. From ancient times until today, items such as stools for chieftains, stamped designs and woven patterns in cloth, brass weights for measuring gold, the sides of jars and bowls and the tops of umbrellas, continue to tell a story or teach a lesson framed in the design of functional, utilitarian devices.

Within the Akan cultures of Ghana and Côte d'Ivoire, the accumulated wisdom and cultural values of a people are evident, remembered and passed along to generations in singular, meaningful imagery of lessons learned throughout the history of the Akan people. The first documented images of the sankofa pictograph (a particular type of adinkra) can be found in R.S. Rattray's book, *Religion and Art in Ashanti* (Oxford, 1927, page 265).

The adinkra which begins the History Chapter is that of a mythical bird, flying forward with its head turned backward, and with an egg in its mouth or with the egg being taken from its back. This symbol reflects the concept of sankofa, the Akan belief that the past serves as a guide for the present and future, that the wisdom in remembering and learning from the past is essential to personal development and growth.

In this technological age, when "knowledge" is freely and sometimes subjectively revised within the time it takes to click on Wikipedia, when new products and immediacy of "present" information increasingly change the way we learn and live, when time is always fleeting and the patient study of the past seems less than relevant to many, is a study of history necessary? Perhaps the following quotes shed a little light on our need to be aware of the past:

> *"Those who cannot remember the past are condemned to repeat it. A country without a memory is a country of madmen."*
> GEORGE SANTAYANA
> (1863–1952, Spanish American philosopher, essayist, poet, and novelist).

> *"History teaches everything including the future."*
> ALPHONSE DE LAMARTINE
> (1790–1869, French poet and politician)

> *"History cannot give us a program for the future, but it can give us a fuller understanding of ourselves, and of our common humanity, so that we can better face the future."*
> ROBERT PENN WARREN
> (1905–1981, Pulitzer Prize winning American novelist, and poet)

> *"If the past has been an obstacle and a burden, knowledge of the past is the safest and the surest emancipation."*
> LORD ACTON
> (1804–1902, English politician, historian, and writer)

> *"If a race has no history, if it has no worthwhile tradition, it becomes a negligible factor in the thought of the world, and it stands in danger of being exterminated."*
> CARTER G. WOODSON
> (1875–1950, African-American historian, author, journalist, and founder of the *Journal of Negro History*, now titled, *The Journal of African-American History*)

> *"Bringing the gifts that my ancestors gave, I am the dream and the hope of the slave. I rise. I rise. I rise."*
> MAYA ANGELOU, "Still I Rise," *And Still I Rise.*

The price of remembering and respecting the lives and lessons of a distant past is far less than the price of knowing no past at all. One of the children with whom I had shared stories and visual arts/writing sessions in an elementary school seemed to be in a sullen mood every day; her grades were poor, and her responses in the classroom were rarely more than sarcastic statements or grunts. One day, as we talked privately, this child told me, "My mother is dead. My father never comes around. My uncle got shot. I live with my grandma. And she doesn't have a story. So I don't have a story, either." What is this child's future, without her cultural history, and with only the difficulties of her present life as a foundation for her existence?

Our personal world views are impacted by our knowledge of what those in our world have experienced; our personal self-confidence and empathy grow from an understanding of and a connection to that world experience. We do not live in the past; we grow from it, to live a worthwhile life in the present.

What we gather and carry from the experiences that are our ancestral knowledge and wisdom, added to what we live and learn, are our sankofa, giving us the confidence to be present and prepared for the path we walk, the life we live, now.

Fourth-generation storyteller ***LYN (LYNETTE) FORD*** *shares from her family's multicultural Affrilachian oral traditions, in folktale adaptations and original stories she calls "Home-Fried Tales". Lyn is an Ohio teaching artist, a storyteller for the Greater Columbus Arts Council's Artists-in-Schools Program, a mentor for young authors and pre-school "writers" for the Thurber Center, and a frequent-flyer who performs and provides workshop presentations across the United States. www.storytellerlynford.com*

The following three articles
"The Civil War: I See it Differently,"
"The Silver Spurs," and
"Historical Storytelling" are meant
as a study from the classroom
teacher and the storytellers' perspectives.
Each professional contributes to
the life of the group of children in
her/his own way. Each has something
unique to say and experience
with the children.

The Civil War

I SEE IT DIFFERENTLY

Kate Anderson McCarthy

OBJECTIVES *for Grade Four*

Students will

- understand the individual's impact on history
- use primary sources to support ideas and project work
- acknowledge multiple perspectives
- acknowledge multiple perspectives about the Civil War

MATERIALS

- R.A.F.T. prompts
- "I Am" prompts
- Civil War primary source documents
- Microsoft Office Publisher

INSTRUCTIONAL PLAN

When I teach an historical event, it is important to me to continuously reinforce the idea of multiple perspectives. In the fall, my fourth grade class studied European settlement in the United States. Throughout, my students looked at events from the viewpoints of both European Settlers and Native Americans as the drama teacher helped them internalize the phrase, "I see it differently."

We continued to use "I see it differently" while studying the Civil War, an essential part of understanding America's past and present identity. At the beginning of the unit, I asked my students to consider differing viewpoints from this era. Their first and most predominate answer was "The North and the South." I told them we would learn a variety of opinions about the Civil War from historians who have biases which shape how they tell history. And, that we would hear about the event from the people who lived it, so that we can think critically about America's Civil War. Critical thinkers entertain many points of view and seek a balanced perspective.

When teaching any subject, but especially Social Studies, I incorporate Wiggins and McTighe's "Six Facets of Understanding" from their book *Understanding by Design*, (Prentice Hall, 1998) for teaching and assessment purposes. These examine the ways students demonstrate mastery of a concept. My goals for students are that they develop empathy and multiple perspectives on the Civil War. Wiggins and McTighe describe these ideas as being inextricably linked, "Students have to learn how to open-mindedly embrace ideas, experiences, and texts that might seem strange, off-putting, or just difficult to access." Wiggins and McTighe define 'perspective' as, "the mature recognition that any answer to a complex question typically involves a point of view." I believe that my students would develop a deep understanding of the multiple perspectives surrounding the Civil War as well as an understanding of individual people's impacts by empathizing with people from both the Union and Confederate sides, as well as looking at history through different lenses created by role, socioeconomic status, race, and gender.

Storyteller Beth Horner came to our classes at the beginning of our unit and told "The Silver Spurs," about Horner's great, great-grandfather, a Confederate soldier who was killed in the Civil War. The only memory her great-grandmother Minnie had of her father was his bright silver spurs, engraved with his last name and the last name of his friend. Decades later, the great-grandson of a Union solider returned the spurs to 80-year-old Minnie, and they both realized his great-grandfather may have stolen the spurs from the dead Confederate soldier, killed at Missionary Ridge. This story touched my students (and me), and was an introduction to the people who fought the war. Students would refer to the story long after Horner left the school.

It also sparked an interest in family stories. So, my students interviewed a family member to learn stories that defined their families, just as the Silver Spurs story did for Horner's family. After hearing "The Silver Spurs" and learning more about their own families' stories, I knew that my students were ready to explore perspectives from the Civil War.

We began with comfortable territory; we learned about the different reasons men had for enlisting in the Union Army. Then, using the R.A.F.T. (Role, Audience, Format, and Topic) format, I asked students to write from the perspective of a Union solider about why he joined the army or to tell about a specific event from the soldier's point of view. Most students were eager to write from the Union perspective, because they viewed these men as heroic. Some of them, however, were able to think more deeply about the Union soldiers and acknowledge that they were not perfect and there were many reasons to join the Union. "In a few months we'll show those rebels what they get when they mess with the Union!" one student wrote, understanding that slavery was not the only reason soldiers wanted to fight, but to preserve the Union as well.

After several writings from this perspective, we began to study the lives of Confederate soldiers. The students had some misconceptions about the Confederate side, believing all of the soldiers were slave-owners. Therefore, they were not as eager to step into their shoes. Yet, student writing reflects a growing understanding of the Confederacy, along with traces of empathy, "I fight [against] a brother for the sake of freedom for the C.S.S.(Confederate Southern States). I fight and I might die, but forever I will live as a soul for the C.S.A." (Confederate States of America) This student acknowledged that Confederate soldiers were proud and fiercely loyal to their cause. Ultimately, the R.A.F.T. writing helped the students recognize that both sides had triumphs and tragedies, as well as divergent viewpoints within their group.

Following two weeks of R.A.F.T. writing from 'soldiers', we moved to develop understanding of those marginalized by society during that era, namely women and African Americans. Looking at how people from different genders, races, and socioeconomic statuses experienced the Civil War, students read a primary or secondary document or an article about a certain person, and then wrote a poem from their perspective using the "I AM" structure. The structure includes prompts that ask students to explore the five senses, as well as one's dreams, fears, pain, hope, and overall identity. Students researched their "person" on the internet and told their stories through powerful poetry, demonstrating an awareness of not only the individual's impact on the war, but the war's impact on individuals.

Name Jesse Date 2/10/10

Brainstorming Sheet

Role: (a Union soldier)
Name: Thomas O'Dean

Audience:
Who am I writing to?
Poem

Format:
Poem or Letter

Topic: Why you are in the Union army
keep the union togther and end Slavery, and mony

The 19 of november 1862
I walked appon the fields of war, My reson twas for union not for Slave. The mony twas good, the Sitting and wating twas not, the Job was bluddy with no fight twas borring. That day when I walked out, there was no dout that I might not retern, and if I did the world would not be the same as that very day when I walked out to kill a brather.

Jesse is a strong creative writer and Civil War aficionado. He relished the opportunity to write from the perspectives of both Union…

Name Jesse Date 2/18/10

Brainstorming Sheet

Role: (a Confederate soldier)
Name: John Beaton

Audience:
Who am I writing to?
Poem

Format:
Poem Letter Journal

Topic: Why are you in the Confederate army?
To fight for the Confedoreate States of Americ,

What is life like as a Confederate soldier?
Not alot of food, Sit, and fight.

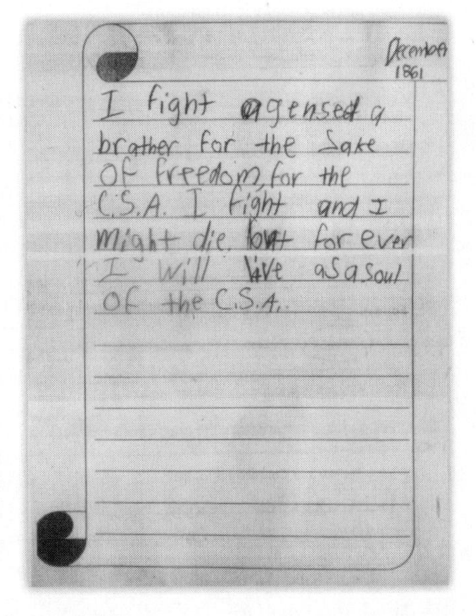

December 1861
I fight agensed a brather for the Sake of freedom, for the C.S.A. I fight and I might die but for ever I will live as a soul of the C.S.A.

… and Confederate soldiers.

I Am

By: Haddie Broughton-DeLong

I am famous
I wonder what is happening in war
I hear boom-boom-boom
I see guns and swords
I want a husband
I am strong
I pretend to be a really man
I feel like a man when I am trying to be one
I touch weapons
I worry about my health
I cried when my husband died
I am brave
I understand why I got taken to prison
I say good and bad things
I dream of us winning war
I try to live my life in my own way
I hope to live long and fight
I am a woman
My name is Amy Clarke and my
boy name is Richard Anderson

I Am

By Catie LaBranche

I am a daughter of a plantation owner
I wonder if the war will be over
I hear gossip about the Union army
I see shot guns
I want the war to end
I am one of the most famous confederates
I pretend that the war is over
I feel bad for the homeless and the wounded
I touch my dresses
I worry about our soldiers
I cry when I hear they died
I am a friend of Jefferson Davis
I understand why we have to fight the war
I say good luck
I dream the war will be over
I try to help the confederates
I hope that the horrid war will be over
I am the daughter of a plantation owner
My name is Mary Chestnut

I Am

By: Nina M. Kaushikkar

I am a woman.
I wonder about what it would be like if women had rights.
I hear the rapid clicking sound the blades of the reaper make.
I see hundreds of reapers in the wheat fields.
I want the world to be a peaceful place.
I am a harvester.
I pretend that I am safe in the fields with others.
I feel the hot air against my skin.
I touch the wheel controlling the reaper.
I worry about how the soldiers are doing.
I cry about how women don't have many rights.
I am a believer.
I understand that the Union men need this, else they get sick.
I say "Good wives! Good women!"
I dream that men will see that women are their equal.
I try to work my hardest.
I hope the war will end soon.
I am a hard worker.
My name is Mary Livermore.

Haddie was able to infer the emotions of Amy Clarke from primary and secondary sources.

Nina loves writing poetry, and her "I Am" poem showcases her empathy for Mary Livermore's struggles and her ability to take on her voice.

Catie was able to step into the shoes of Mary Chesnut and use descriptive language to convey experiences and emotions.

Culminating our study of the Civil War, we were visited by Syd Lieberman, who told his story "Abraham and Isaac: Sacrifice at Gettysburg." This story wove Lincoln's "Gettysburg Address" with the story of a Union foot soldier Isaac Taylor. The emotion resonated with my students; students expressed empathy for Lincoln's sadness and Taylor's thrill of the fight. They appreciated the story of the Gettysburg Address and understood the motives, action and characters presented. My students sympathized with characters from stories they read in primary source documents as well, and Syd's story helped them go beyond learning about battles and generals to examine the humanity in the war. They finished the unit with an understanding of why this war began, different perspectives on the war, and how the war shaped our country.

ASSESSMENT

To assess my students' understanding of multiple perspectives, of how individuals impacted the Civil War, and of how primary source documents can be used to learn about history, I required each student to create a Civil War newspaper. As in their R.A.F.T. writing, they had to decide who their audience was. Their audience would determine the title of their newspapers, their topics, as well as the perspective they took when writing their articles. Every student had to include an article about a battle, a general, an arts and culture piece, advertisements, political cartoons, and an opinion-editorial, or op-ed piece, which was to be written after reading a primary source document.

When evaluating students' newspapers, the students' choices about their audience were important; their choice to write from a Northern, Southern, or neutral perspective often reflected the depth of their understanding of the Civil War. I looked to see that their articles were accurate, and that they represented a specific voice. For instance, a newspaper written for the South should represent the Confederate viewpoint. The students' op-ed pieces revealed a great deal about their understanding of the Civil War and multiple perspectives. They were able to step into the shoes of a person who lived hundreds of years ago with authentic emotion, revealing their empathy for those on both the Union and Confederates sides of the conflict.

The Corny Potato Weekly

Volume 7
Issue 134

THOUSANDS OF SOLDIERS KILLED AT GETTYSBURG

Mail comments to: The Corny Potato Weekly, PO box 6356351651,Chicago, IL

By Ben Ballmer

Probably the biggest battle so far in this war started in Gettysburg. It all started when General Lee tried to march north up to Washington DC. The Union had defenses in Gettysburg that were easily overrun. General Meade sent the Union army to intercept him. They met in Gettysburg. That was when the battle began.

The Union army was pushed back to Cemetery Hill, Culp's Hill, and Cemetery Ridge. The Confederates prepared to attack from Seminary Ridge. On the second day, fighting broke out. At the end of the day, the Confederates had nearly surrounded Meade's men. Lee decided to send General Pickett to finish him off. Pickett led a charge of 6000 men at Meade's men. The Union's forces were more spaced out and defeated Pickett's. Lee, who had lost a third of his army, retreated. The Union won.

A map of Pickett's charge

A picture of Pickett's charge

The compromise being made

"The compromise of 1850 is one of the Results of his actions from 1820 to now to make both the north and the south happy"

HENRY CLAY MAKES COMPROMISE OF 1850

The only reason that the North ... haven't been ... make the North and the South both happy.

The Compromise ... California a free state ...

His first compromise, The Missouri Compromise of 1820 (which, as you can tell by the name, was made 50 years ago) made Maine a free state and Missouri a slave state. It also drew an imaginary line ... Missouri. All states ... were Free ...

MCCLELLAN CHICKENS OUT

Everyone thought that General George Brinton McClellan had potential. They were quickly proved wrong. Born in Philadelphia in 1826, McClellan graduated second in his West Point class, and served in the Mexican War.

After firing General McDowell, Lincoln decided that McClellan would make a fine general. That was a big mistake. Everyone was happy when he won the battle of Rich Mountain. Lincoln then ordered him to attempt to take Richmond. On the way there he drew general Johnston in the Battle of Seven Pines. General Lee realized that McClellan was trying to take Richmond and prepared the defenses. When McClellan arrived, Lee was waiting. The Seven Days Battles ensued and McClellan was sure that he was outnumbered 2 to 1. Eventually, he chickened out, retreated, and the confederates won.

Later on, in the Battle of the Antietam. When Lee's forces retreated, McClellan didn't pursue them across the river. Lincoln met with him at Antietam and said he was fired.

McClellan then became a democratic candidate in the election of 1864, running against Lincoln. Lincoln won the election with 55% of the votes. McClellan the retired from his career in politics—by Ben Ballmer

George Brinton McClellan

A LOOK AT HOMER

Throughout this Civil War, there hasn't been anyone who can't identify the drawing style of Winslow Homer. He began his art career when he was apprenticed to a commercial lithographer. In 1850 he got a job at Harper's Weekly drawing pictures for newspaper articles. Later on, he started a career as a painter, painting pictures like "The Sharpshooter" and "Prisoners From the Front." His paintings are currently a big cultural influence—by Ben Ballmer

"Later on, he started a career as a painter, painting pictures like The Sharpshooter and Prisoners From the Front"

Winslow Homer

"The Sharpshooter" by Winslow Homer

"Prisoners from the Front" by Winslow Homer

Page 2

The Corny Potato Weekly

KENTUCKY BOURBON WHISKEY

MEN WANTED FOR THE NAVY!

Military Goods.

WHAT ARE WE

... fighting in ... find the ... but necessary for peace.

When the Mexican American war was over there was peace. Every war in History ended with peace.

This war will end with peace too if we win it. We must give our enemy what they asked for! This is why we must fight, for peace.

War will always, eventually become peace

-by William T. Sherman

William T. Sherman

Ben's newspaper not only features multiple perspectives, it is infused with his comedic voice.

OPPOSITE PAGE
Levi is a student fascinated with the Civil War and passionate about social justice. While he personally sided with the Union, he challenged himself to write a newspaper from the Confederate perspective.

Volume 9 Issue 67

Feb 9

The Southern Politics and War Weekly

THE BATTLE OF PETERSBURG

INSIDE THIS ISSUE:

One of the most exciting and intense battles of this war has just recently ended! Grant made a daring move to get past the Confederate troops. He made it so the Confederates lost track of him.

Then, Grant took his troops to the Appomattox River. His engineers built pontoon bridges and got into Petersburg, Virginia and attacked the Confederate troops from behind.

Also the reason why this battle was important was: It wasn't just a battle it was more. Grant did one of the first sneak attacks. I'm sad to say but the Union will win this war.

CALHOUN CRUSHES ANTI-SLAVERY BELIEVERS

By Levi Goldman For the Politics and Weekly...

pro slavery senator. He tried to make slavery everywhere. He did that until he died.

reason why the government passed the fugitive slave law was to make Calhoun happy.

Finally, he was born in

THE SPRINGFIELD RIFLE

most favored weapons of both sides. But it is one of the most expensive. On both sides the price is twenty dollars from the armory!

The Springfield rifle

THE MONITOR AND MERRIMACK

of the most exciting and strangest battle that happened! Confederates built a ship called the ... to get past ... blockade ... Confederate ... the ship tore through the blockade. The Union copied us and built their own ironclad. It wasn't as strong as ours but it still was powerful. It was called the Monitor. Both ships dueled neither won but we tore through the Union blockade. Since we tore through the blockade we could win this war!

...ST: NORTHERN VILLAIN

...'s trying to ...very! We ...very to ... and also created that despicable image of Uncle Sam. He's truly a villain!

The villain Thomas Nast above

ADS AND CARTOONS

Grant is the most feared General. He himself attacked the great Robert E. Lee! With him, sadly, they might win the war. Grant's biggest victory was against Lee when he captured Petersburg.

Also he captured Chattanooga, Tennessee. He took over as head commander for McClellan. McClellan was a worse commander then Grant ... probably would hav... war.

He also made it so no... of the battles are here i... south. Grant has definit... turned the tide of this wa...

WAR HISTORY

This a general overview of the war so far. It all started with our states rights. That terrible Union did not give us good rights and they wanted to stop slavery!

We succeeded! We fired at Fort Sumter.

Then the war began. We are winning lots of battles.

Those Union G...als don't know ...thing. With our ... success the war is ... our hands!

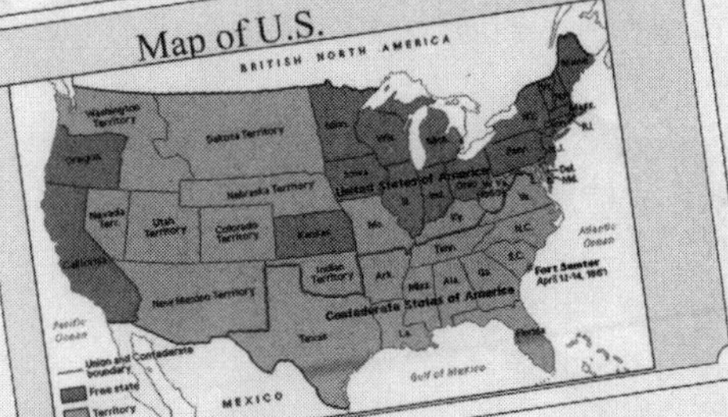

Op-Ed

I have fought in two wars and even though war can be bad it can help improve the country and can be necessary for peace.

It was necessary to stop your rebellion. So when I went into the south and burnt down those cities it was for peace.

All the various Union Generals who made those "brutal" attacks were all for peace.

So I think this war was necessary for peace.

Bio: General William T. Sherman fought in the War of Northern Aggression and the Mexican War

RESOURCES

Ford, Carin T. *Daring Women of the Civil War.* Berkeley Heights, NJ: Enslow Publishers, 2004.

Haskins, James. *Black, Blue, and Gray: an African American in the Civil War.* NY: Simon & Schuster Books for Young Readers, 1998.

Horner, Beth. *The Silver Spurs: A True Tale of the American Civil War.* DVD. Evanston, IL: Beth Horner, 2002.

Lewis Patrick J. *The Brothers' War: Civil War Voices in Verse.* Washington, D.C.: National Geographic, 2007.

Lieberman, Adrienne and Syd. *Abraham and Isaac: Sacrifice at Gettysburg.* CD. Evanston, IL: Syd Leiberman, 2008.

Silverman, Jerry. *Songs and Stories of the Civil War.* Brookfield, CT: Twenty-First Century Books, 2002.

www.ket.org/civilwar/primary.html.

Wiggins, Grant and McTighe, Jay. *Understanding by Design.* Alexandria, VA: ASCD, 2008.

KATE ANDERSON McCARTHY *began her teaching career at a charter school in Chicago before coming to the Baker Demonstration School in Wilmette, Illinois, where she has taught fourth and fifth grade for four years. Kate's different experiences in schools led to her interest in creating dynamic curriculum to meet students' individual needs, strengths and interests. Kate holds a bachelor's degree in English from Lake Forest College and a master's of arts in teaching degree from National-Louis University. She is currently pursuing her master's of education degree in curriculum and instruction with a concentration on English Language Learners.*

The Silver Spurs

SMALL MOMENTS IN THE MOSH PIT OF THE LARGE HISTORICAL EVENT

Beth Horner

"The Silver Spurs" is set in the chaos and tragedy of the American Civil War. It takes a large scaled historical event and brings it home through small moments in a very specific, personal, yet universal episode that is impactful today.

The Story

"The Silver Spurs" is the story of *my father* telling me the story of four-year old Minnie who watches *her father*, Wesley Winans, leave for the Civil War in 1861. On his boots are a set of engraved silver spurs. Minnie's father is killed in Chattanooga, Tennessee and never returns home to her. His body is never recovered. His war diary returns via a fellow soldier and through it, Minnie comes to understand the hardship of war and how desperately her father tried to get home to her. Sixty years after the war, the silver spurs are discovered in a dusty glass case in a mom-and-pop restaurant in Iowa. They are returned to an aged Minnie, who for the first time since she was four years old, finds a bit of peace about her father's devastating death. In closing the story, I tell of meeting my 96-year old great-grandmother Minnie when I was four years old and of my father's words each time he told me the story: *The grief of war is not only visited on those who fight and die, Bethy-Beth, but also on their families, sometimes for generations to come.*

I accompany the story with a Civil War song and reveal photos of Minnie and her father Winans at the end of the story.

Three thoughts come to mind when I think about telling "The Silver Spurs" to students:

1. History is made up of people.

Dates, places and names are the skeletal structures that comprise an historical event. However, it is the people who live it, existing without the hindsight or multi-perspectives of later historians, who make up its flesh, blood, muscle, gray matter, heart, bowels and breath. Furthermore, history is lived out by *ordinary people*, often flawed and often just trying to survive. It is the every day person down in the mosh pit of an historical event who is hit with its full impact. As a storyteller, I believe it is my job to tell the story of the mosh pit experience in order to truly bring an understanding of that historical event and its impact to my listeners.

The Facts: The Civil War is an extremely complex and horrific but decisive event in America's history that had a huge and lasting impact on our society. More Americans died than in any other war. Over 620,000 soldiers died, thousands more were permanently wounded and thousands more lived the rest of their lives with Soldier's Heart (now called Post Traumatic Stress Disorder). Fought on our own soil, thousands more people were killed, wounded and permanently displaced. Most significant, it brought about the end of legal slavery in the U.S.

Personalizing the Facts: Through "The Silver Spurs," I wanted to bring this large, complex event into sharp focus, to communicate the everyday person's universal experience of the war. To do so, I decided to personalize the war via the story of a very specific soldier and his family.

I have ancestors who fought on both sides of the Civil War. However, I was most struck by the power behind Minnie's story, by her soldier father's experience (as related through his diary which I had read), by my memory of the aged Minnie whom I had met when I was a girl, and by the spurs themselves that I had held in my own hands. These intense, even tactile memories were vivid pieces of any soldier's story, any family's story and thus, of the bowels of the war itself.

2. *Part of raising children is helping them think critically about their individual daily lives and their lives within a larger society.*

Citizens must understand that historical and present events exist in a context and must be understood or acted upon as such. History is not cut and dried. History is complicated, multi-faceted, messy and must be considered within any number of contextual relationships.

My six-year old nephew once asked me a long series of questions, each beginning with "Who are the good guys and who are the bad guys?" and continuing with "Democrats or Republicans?...Police or prisoners?...Parents or kids?...Snakes or rats?"...and on and on. I attempted to explain that neither was all good nor all bad and that it depended upon one's life experience and point of view. He became impatient. He was simply trying to order his world and could not absorb the subtleties.

With all that life throws at us (certainly at young people), we often revert to that six-year old desire for a cut and dried world. It is intellectually and emotionally exhausting to wade through the messiness of multiple layers, varying perspectives, emotionally charged prior experiences, cultural backgrounds and shades of truth to make informed decisions about our present and our future. It is our job as educators and storytellers to provide students, future voting citizens, with the tools necessary to do so—to raise critical thinkers. Telling a universal story of an everyday person's experience in an historical event that greatly impacted our society is one way to guide a student toward thinking critically.

I immediately faced a dilemma when I began writing "The Silver Spurs": I felt uncomfortable with the fact that Winans, my ancestor and one of my protagonists, had fought for the Confederacy. Even though Winans was not fully behind the southern cause and was reluctant to fight and even though my primary motivation was to write of a universal experience in a soldier's life and the life of his family, I was uneasy. In school, I was taught that the Civil War was fought solely over the issue of slavery. All Caucasian people in the south were pro-slavery; all in the north against it. There was a war. The good guys won. Everyone lived happily ever after. Until I conducted research for this story, if my nephew had asked me his good/bad question, I would have confidently answered: "Northerners good. Southerners bad." End of story.

I became hesitant to tell their story, but I knew that Minnie's and Winans' specific experience of war was universal. So, I decided to go ahead and conduct research. I went to Chattanooga where Winans was killed and I stayed with a storytelling colleague. I revealed my dilemma to him. My colleague said to me:

"My ancestors lived on a tiny farm in Tennessee and never even considered the idea of slavery. All they knew was that one day, Union soldiers raided their farm, burned their crops and house, stole their livestock, killed their father when he tried to defend his family and left them with no way to survive. The sons, all teenagers, joined the Confederate Army. There was no question as to whether or not to "go to war". The war came to their doorstep and was thrust upon them. I am glad that the South lost and that slavery was ended, but I was raised being told that the Civil War was "The War of Northern Aggression."

His lecture was eye opening to me. Who is good? Who is bad? Why does one do what one does? Life isn't so simple down in the mosh pit.

So, I continued to craft the story of Minnie and her father Winans, focusing on the universal story lines:

a) a little girl with no concept of war except that her father leaves and never returns, and

b) a soldier who reluctantly leaves the family and home he loves, uncertain of his future or their future, to fight for a "cause" he does not fully understand, eventually coming to realize it is more complex than he ever imagined.

3. *A powerfully constructed tale of an historical event is comprised of broad strokes broken down into small, "drop away" moments that produce potent, unforgettable visuals in the listener's mind.*

Vivid images create emotional responses in the listener's heart. My goal as a storyteller is to create images so vivid that they pop up on the computer screen of the listener's memory each time he or she thinks of that historical event, reactivating those emotional responses. Therefore, when telling a story of an historical event, I focus on very specific, very personal, very vivid experiences within the larger event.

I always begin story construction with broad strokes: the scope of the story, the book report, the facts. I then do what I call "break it down, break it down, break it down" or "zoom in, zoom in, zoom in" to small moments, what I term as "drop away moments." Dates and places are important, but small moments bring it home to the heart of the listener.

A "drop away moment" is a moment in the story when all else falls away from the story and the listener's mind except that one instant in time and the image associated with it. The story zooms in like a camera lens so that nothing else is seen or experienced by the listener but that one moment. My intent is for the listener to linger over that living, breathing moment, as if frozen in time, and to take the resulting image into his or her heart.

Her name was Minnie. She was four years old when her father tossed her into the air, gave her a great big hug and set her down onto the lane. Standing in the lane, she watched as her father turned away from her, walked down the lane, got up onto his horse, slowly looked back at her with a sad smile, turned again and rode off to fight in a war. "Now you know, Bethy Beth," my father would say when he told me the story, "when you are only four years old, what you remember is very close to the ground. What little Minnie remembered of her father were the silver spurs he wore on his boots, for they shone in the sunlight and jangled as he walked down the lane.

****

The two men stood there for the longest time in silence—each holding one spur—each realizing that one man's grandfather had stolen the silver spurs from the other man's grandfather's dead body. Two men, standing in silence, bonded together by their grandfathers who had been sworn enemies.

****

When her son placed what was left of those silver spurs into her aged hands, she looked down at them for the longest time, opening her hands, closing them, opening them, then clutching the spurs over her heart—a bit of her father returned at last. Her son later said that at that moment—and for only a moment—he saw a kind of peace pass over his mother's face that he had never seen before.

Actual words such as diary entries and letter excerpts heighten a "drop away moment."

> *June 26, 1862. Today I received a letter from my wife Jane. Ah, those three words that sum up all bliss: "my wife Jane". Oh my wife, my children, how grateful to my hungry heart is a letter from home. Like balm to a wound, ice to thirst, consolation to a wounded spirit, wine to one ready to faint.*

The last entry in the diary was written in a different hand:

> *On this day, the 25th of November, 1863, at the battle of Missionary Ridge, Chattanooga, Tennessee, Colonel Wesley Winans was shot. He walked to the bottom of the hill, by the assistance of a friend. The surgeon there told him that his wound was mortal. His last words: "My regiment has acted gallantly today. This will kill my poor wife." The Federals were pressing our folks and we were obliged to fall back. I removed this diary from his coat so that one of those who served under and loved him, should they be passing that way, could return his words to his beloved wife. We leaned him against a tree, saluted as we marched by, and left him there, not yet dead.*
>
> *Body not recovered.*

Photographs also create a "drop away moment." At the end of *The Silver Spurs*, I reveal two things:

a) that Minnie was my great grandmother whom I met when I was 4 years old and she was 96, and

b) large photos of Minnie and Wesley Winans.

Both revelations zoom the story into sharp focus. Often an audible intake of breath occurs at these moments of revelation because the photos instantly and powerfully move the story from the abstract to the very real: these people were real, this war was real, and its impact was real.

A high school student in Ottawa, Illinois wrote to me: "I never thought about war having real people in it. I thought it was like a videogame. After you came to our school, I started watching the news."

Stories from the past tell us who we are by telling us who we were. A good historical story shows the complex historical context and the many forces or perspectives that people—down in the mosh pit—faced. A great historical story permanently transports the facts into the listener's heart through memorable images. There is no better avenue for students to understand the interconnectedness of past and present and to understand the everyday person's role in shaping the future.

MINNIE DUBOSE WINANS HORNER: 1857–1955
Photo taken: Montrose, Louisiana, ca. 1865.
Daughter of Jane Harper Winans and Wesley Parker Winans. Great grandmother to Beth Horner.

WESLEY PARKER WINANS: 1825 – 1863
Photo taken: Shreveport, Louisiana, 1861.
Father of Minnie Winans, Great-great grandfather to Beth Horner. Killed at battle of Missionary Ridge, Chattanooga, Tennessee, November 23, 1863. His Silver Spurs and his Civil War Diary remain in the family.

Storyteller ***BETH HORNER*** *is a former librarian, having worked at the Yale University and Champaign, Illinois Public Libraries. A National Storytelling Network Circle of Excellence Award recipient, she has performed on Live From National Geographic, at the National Storytelling Festival, conducted workshops for NASA and the National Council of Teachers of English, and served on the National Storytelling Association's Board of Directors. In addition to touring, Beth most recently worked with the NASA/ Johnson Space Center's Story Mining project, collecting stories from the scientists behind the Apollo Space Missions. www.bethhorner.com*

Historical Storytelling

Adrienne and Syd Lieberman

When Jane Stenson asked me to tell "Abraham and Isaac: Sacrifice at Gettysburg" at the Baker Demonstration School in Wilmette, Illinois, I hesitated. My audience would be 4th and 5th graders.

My wife Adrienne and I knew we had created a moving and meaningful story. It received standing ovations when I told it around the country, and it was awarded the Story Magazine Gold Award for 2009. But we considered it a piece for adults. I could envision telling the story to high school and junior high school students, but 4th and 5th graders? Little did I know the sway it would hold over these young students.

An Elusive Story

Two years earlier, Adrienne and I had decided to write a piece for Lincoln's 2008 bicentennial. We quickly focused on Gettysburg and Lincoln's Gettysburg Address. These were turning points in the war and in our country's history. After all, Lincoln's speech after this seminal battle in 1863 pointed America toward fulfilling the stirring promise of the Declaration of Independence that all men were created equal.

But it hadn't been easy to create. So much has been written about Lincoln and the Gettysburg Address. We read and Xeroxed, then read and Xeroxed some more. An early working plan was to divide the story into three parts: Lincoln, the Battle of Gettysburg, and the speech. We soon began to spin out drafts on Lincoln's early life; the history of Gettysburg; and the address, which many people consider to be the greatest speech in American history.

Needed: One Good Man

But something was missing. The 40,000 dead and wounded soldiers at Gettysburg saddened us, but Lincoln's speech honoring them remained lofty and abstract.

"What we need," said Adrienne, "is to personalize Lincoln's words about the soldiers' sacrifice. How about a soldier who fought and died at Gettysburg?"

Unsure about how to locate such a character, she scoured the shelves of the Evanston Library looking for Civil War books.

That day she toted home a bulging bag. One book seemed especially promising. Adrienne chose *The Last Full Measure* because its title—a phrase from the Gettysburg Address—suggested that it would center on the Battle of Gettysburg. The author, Richard Moe, wrote about The First Minnesota Volunteers, a regiment that served in almost every major battle in the east during the Civil War's first three years. In the Battle of Gettysburg, the First Minnesota lost as many as 178 of its 300 soldiers in a sacrificial mission that turned the tide of this battle in the Union's favor.

The book's cover featured a picture of two soldiers from the First Minnesota Volunteers. We would later discover that one of them was Isaac Taylor. The other was his brother Henry.

Time Traveling

Moe's book included selected letters and journal entries from the Taylor brothers and their fellow Minnesota soldiers. Isaac, one of the Minnesota First's most faithful writers, began his diary in earnest on New Year's Day, 1862.

Isaac's tongue-in-cheek first entry thanked the assumed finder of the diary in advance for returning it to his family in the event of his death:

> *TO WHOM IT MAY CONCERN.*
> *MR. SECESH;*
>
> *Please forward this diary to J.H. Taylor, Prairie City, McDonough Co., Illinois. By doing so, you will exhibit your magnanimity, accommodativeness & divers other virtues, besides conferring no small favor on a defunct individual.*
>
> *Yours truly,*
> *I.L. TAYLOR*
> *High Private of Co. E*
> *1st Reg. Minnesota Vol.*

Adrienne immediately fell in love with Isaac, regaling me with one diary entry after another. Isaac wrote about the hijinks and boredom that constitute a soldier's life, of the weather and the books he was reading, and of his and Henry's experience as prisoners of war. Most movingly of all, he described his eagerness to "put a quietus on this infernal rebellion."

On July 1, 1863, Isaac and Henry were camped near Gettysburg, awaiting the decisive battle that would take place the next day. They made coffee and ate hardtack before spreading their blankets and trying to sleep, but eager anticipation of the next day's battle kept them awake.

Isaac was one of the many Minnesota soldiers who fell in that day's battle. The First Minnesota was asked to charge a force three times their size, but the seasoned veterans of this regiment understood that their sacrifice might save the battle and the war for the Union.

Adrienne wept while reading Henry's mournful description of finding and burying Isaac's body the morning after the battle. We had found our soldier.

The Bible Tells Us So

Fortuitously, his name was Isaac. We had always considered the Bible story of Abraham and Isaac a troubling tale. How could Abraham, a loving father, think that God would have demanded he sacrifice his beloved son? How could a loving God tell a father to do this? And how could we admire the character of a man who failed to question such a directive?

Adrienne had never before encountered a satisfying explanation of this story. Now, she thought, if we could picture Abraham Lincoln as a spiritual father of our country—the soldiers, after all, called him Father Abraham—and Isaac as one of the thousands of "sons" who must be sacrificed to save the Union, we had the underpinning of our story. Even though our pair never met, our story would turn them into a father and his son, and show the terrible sacrifice the father had to justify to a grieving nation.

Mining Isaac's Diary

We poured over a copy of Isaac's transcribed and edited diary, which had been published in 1944 in a journal called *Minnesota History* by a scholar named Hazel Wolf. At Northwestern University Library, we read and copied Isaac's journal. We studied each day of Isaac's two-year path to Gettysburg, choosing what to include and mourning the many details we had to omit. We chuckled at Isaac's keen delight to spy into the Hall of Representatives in Washington and his hunger for fresh meat and fruit to supplement the soldier's dried rations. But most all, we hoped to capture his deepest hunger: to help save the union.

A Young Audience Responds

Would young students appreciate let alone understand this complex, sad story? I shortened the piece a little, but didn't change any of the language. The last thing I wanted was to dumb down the story. I taught high school English for 30 years and found that students never backed away from difficult material presented honestly.

The students listened quietly, but I still couldn't be sure that they understood it. Afterwards, I told them that I wanted to ask some questions to see how well they comprehended the story. I could sense their excitement at this suggestion.

I began by asking some general questions about Lincoln and Isaac Taylor. They recognized that Lincoln's life had been filled with death and that he cared for the soldiers and didn't want them to die. They knew that it was difficult for him to send soldiers into battle. They had connected to Lincoln's character.

The same was true for Isaac Taylor. They saw that he really wanted to be a good soldier and save the union. And they were saddened that he died at the battle of Gettysburg, his big chance to fight. Their answers about both figures were filled with empathy.

History Comes Alive

Then I turned my attention to the Gettysburg Address, a short but challenging speech. The students grasped Lincoln's point that this country was founded on principles of freedom and universal equality, and that the Civil War was being fought about these principles.

They also understood that Lincoln felt that the ground at Gettysburg was special because of what the soldiers had done there. It was interesting that I didn't have to define dedicated, consecrated or hallow. The context provided their meanings.

The students even comprehended the toughest part of the speech, where Lincoln explains what he wants his listeners to do. In this section, the syntax and sentence structure are somewhat convoluted, but, as I took them through it phrase by phrase, I could see that they understood that Lincoln wanted his listeners to make the soldiers' deaths meaningful.

One student even connected the end of the speech, an appeal that "government of the people, by the people, and for the people...not perish from the earth," with the speech's beginning. He saw that the government Lincoln was talking about at the end of the address was the government that the war was being fought over.

The student who volunteered that answer struggled to find the right words. It was fascinating to watch. He understood the story, but he couldn't easily express his insight. Eventually he found the words he was looking for. You could see the pride on his face.

On one hand, I was astonished. This was difficult material. On the other, I wasn't. The students understood the Gettysburg Address because of the story that had preceded it. Through story, they traveled to another time and place and returned with an understanding of this important piece of history.

I don't think they could have appreciated the speech without the story.

__ADRIENNE__ and Syd collaborated to create "Abraham and Isaac; Sacrifice at Gettysburg and Summer of Treason: Philadelphia 1776." During a 25-year career as a childbirth educator, Adrienne wrote or co-wrote five books and dozens of articles on birth and parenting. She also wrote numerous chapters and features for middle school social studies textbooks. Adrienne is currently a satisfied freelance medical writer, a cheerful story listener, a devoted volunteer architectural tour guide, and an ecstatic grandmother.

__SYD LIEBERMAN__ is an internationally acclaimed storyteller, an author, and an award-winning teacher. His storytelling has garnered awards from American Library Association, Parent's Choice, and Storytelling World. Syd has taught storytelling at the Kennedy Center and Disney World; received commissions from the Smithsonian Institution, NASA, Historic Philadelphia, and Johnstown, Pennsylvania; and performed at the US Holocaust Museum. Syd's work has won him a place in the National Storytelling Network's Circle of Excellence. He has also received the Golden Apple Award for excellence in teaching from the Golden Apple Foundation. www.sydlieberman.com

Exploring the Great Depression

VISUAL ART, CREATIVE WRITING AND STORYTELLING

Sherry Norfolk

OBJECTIVES *for Middle School*

Students will

- research, write and perform stories that accurately portray the impact of the Great Depression.

MATERIALS

- "Out of Work" by Aimee Schweig
- research material on the Great Depression (internet resources and library resources)

OUT OF WORK by Aimee Schweig, Missouri History Museum, St Louis.

A few years ago, the Missouri History Museum invited my husband, Bobby, and me to work with the Reading Bias/Writing Tolerance: Using History's Powerful Stories project (http://www.biasandtolerance.org), working with middle school students to develop historical narratives based on the Great Depression. Our three-day project included viewing visual artwork, creating collaborative historical fiction narratives, developing these into performance pieces, and culminated in a final performance for funders and educators.

INSTRUCTIONAL PLAN

Before we met the students, they had learned about the Great Depression and had toured the Reading Bias/Writing Tolerance exhibit at the Museum. In particular, they were asked to look at the painting "Out of Work" by Aimee Schweig (http://www.biasandtolerance.org/gallery.php#). After viewing and discussing it, the class created a tableau of the painting, re-creating the postures, positions, and facial expressions of the men pictured. The students commented on the emotions evoked by simply assuming these poses.

Then the concept of historical fiction was introduced. (Creating a historical fiction story requires knowledge of the time period, including historical, geographical, environmental information. Weaving facts into a fictionalized story = historical fiction.) Students worked in small groups, choosing one of the men as their subject, and developing a story about him, including the answers to these questions:

1. Which man did you choose (describe his clothing and what he looks like, including his emotional state)
2. Give him a name.
3. What kind of job does he have or did he have?
4. Does he have a wife, children, and/or parents to support? Describe his family.
5. Where does he live?
6. What has happened to him or is about to happen?
7. What is he worried about? (health of family member, losing house, children's education, etc.)
8. What will he do to solve his problem?

As students began their work, they typically focused on the storyline, not giving much regard to historical accuracy or authenticity; however, once their stories began to take shape, my job was to ask them lots of questions, helping them see the relevance of researching for specific information that would make their stories more meaningful. Then I was able to guide them to research material on the internet and in the library in order to find historical facts to weave into their narratives. Gradually, their fiction stories began to genuinely reflect the time period.

Once the narratives were complete, the groups began to develop their stories into performance pieces. While all members were required to participate, they were given lots of options: one person could narrate while the others acted out the story; each member could be assigned a role and speaking parts; some could provide sound effects or sing period songs while others act or narrate, etc. Rehearsals with instructor feedback allowed them to explore their options and prepare for performance.

Before the final performance, the groups performed for each other in class with students and instructors providing positive feedback. This opportunity for peer-teaching was invaluable—not only did students gain confidence from the comments, but they learned more about the time period and about ways to improve their own performances.

As students moved through this lesson, they became invested in learning about the time period, and genuinely began to empathize with the plights of the people who lived through it. They spontaneously connected those times with the economic situation we are currently facing in the U.S., comparing and contrasting governmental responses then and now and strategizing more effective outcomes. These discussions erupted during the collaborative phase, but were also part of the peer response during performances.

ASSESSMENT

Use the Essential Skills rubric to assess students'...

1. Data-gathering skills
   - Acquire information by observation.
   - Locate information from a variety of sources.
   - Compile. Organize, and evaluate information.
   - Extract and interpret information.
   - Communicate orally and in writing.

2. Intellectual skills
   - Compare things, ideas, events, and situations on the basis of similarities and differences.
   - Ask appropriate and searching questions.
   - Draw conclusions or inferences from evidence.
   - Arrive at general ideas.
   - Make sensible predictions from generalizations.

3. Decision-making skills. Learning to:
   - Consider alternative decisions.
   - Consider the consequences of each solution.
   - Make decisions and justify them in relationship to democratic principles.
   - Act based on those decisions.

4. Interpersonal skills. Learning to:
   - See things from the point of view of others.
   - Understand one's own beliefs, feelings, abilities, and shortcomings and how they affect relations with others.
   - Use group generalizations without stereotyping and arbitrarily classifying individuals.
   - Work effectively with others as a group member.
   - Give and receive constructive criticism.
   - Accept responsibility and respect the rights and property of others.

RESOURCES

Northern Kentucky University. *I will survive: family life and the Great Depression.* http://www.nku/~eng/history/familylife.html

Wessel's Living History Farm. Farming in the 1930s. http://www.livinghistoryfarm.org/farminginthe1930s/farminginthe1930s Great links to even more information.

Farrell, Jacqueline. *The Great Depression.* San Diego, CA: Lucent Books, 1996.

Fremon, David K. *The Great Depression in American History.* Springfield, NJ: Enslow Publishers, 1997.

Lacey, Bill. *Depression Soup Kitchen,* 1933. Carlsbad, CA: Interact Publishers, Inc., 1995.

Mulvey, Deb, ed. *We Had Everything But Money.* New York: Crescent Books, 1992.

Nishi, Dennis. *Life During the Great Depression.* San Diego, CA: Lucent Books, 1998.

***SHERRY NORFOLK** is an award-winning, internationally acclaimed storyteller and teaching artist, and one of the co-authors, co-editors of this book! See complete bio at the end of the book.*

Day of Remembrance

Alton Chung

OBJECTIVES *for Grades Four – Eight*

Students will:

- articulate the reasons why people of Japanese ancestry living in the United States at the outbreak of World War II were removed from their homes on the West Coast and were incarcerated in camps throughout the US.
- develop empathy regarding the attitudes, values, and behaviors of the Japanese Americans during World War II.
- develop critical thinking skills and discernment with regards to stories with conflicting points of view.
- use knowledge of facts and concepts along with ethical and moral implications drawn from history to make informed decisions and to take action on current issues confronting society.

MATERIALS

Chung, Alton W. *Okage Sama De (I am what I am because of you.)* DVD Alton Chung, 2008.

INSTRUCTIONAL PLAN

Stories allow children to access and assimilate information on a variety of levels. Through narrative, the impact of large, complex, historically significant events can be distilled down to their effect on a single individual. Children can receive and internalize a person's story and therefore gain a framework through which they experience the entire event and establish context.

Each year, on or about February 19, Japanese American communities gather to commemorate a Day of Remembrance with speeches, stories, and lectures on civil rights. On February 19, 1942, President Franklin D. Roosevelt signed Executive Order 9066, authorizing the removal of any persons from any location for the security of the United States. This cleared the way for the relocation of Japanese Americans to the internment camps.

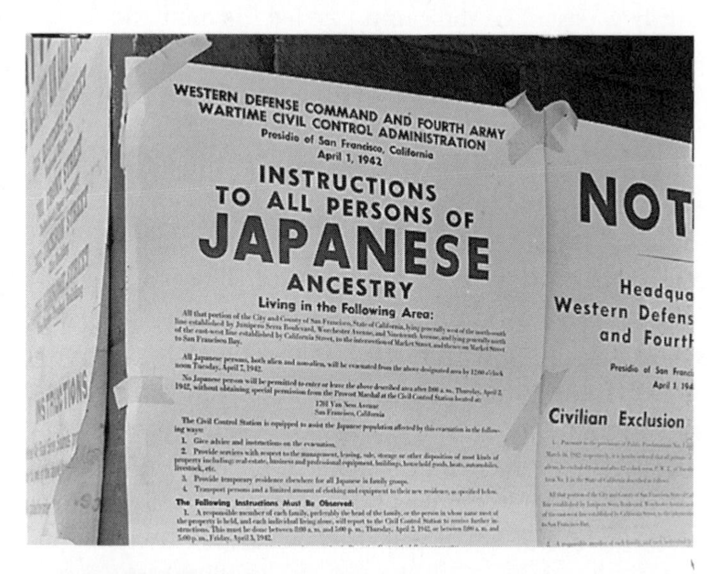

ORDER-POSTING: Exclusion Order posted at First and Front Streets directing removal of persons of Japanese ancestry from the first San Francisco section to be effected by the evacuation

THE HIRANO FAMILY, left to right, George, Hisa, and Yasbei. Colorado River Relocation Center, Poston, Arizona, 1942–1945

Ted Tanouye was drafted into the army after Pearl Harbor. He joined the 100th Battalion/442nd Regimental Combat Team, the all Japanese American unit, and was eventually awarded the Medal of Honor posthumously. In telling this story, I touch upon the forced evaluation and internment. I describe what it was like to have to pack up what you can carry and move into a horse stall at an assembly center and then to an internment camp. Even though Ted's family was sent to the camps, he led his men and fought with incredible courage. In 1944, although severely wounded, he single-handedly captured an entire German-occupied hill in Italy and was awarded the Distinguished Service Cross. In 2000, the service commendations of many Asian Americans were reviewed due to the pervasive prejudice during WWII and Ted's DSC, was elevated to the Medal of Honor.

Children may not understand the complexity of the situation, but they are in tune with the feelings of unfairness and injustice. They can identify with acts of courage and selflessness. Children with special needs, those with behavior disabilities, and those for whom English is a second language, may not be able to fully articulate the concepts and facts, but they can resonate with the feelings of redemption, honor, and gratitude evoked by the story.

One parent told me after a performance that her son was mildly autistic and had some behavioral problems. He was fidgety and she was thinking that they might have to leave, but when the story began her son stopped fidgeting, leaned forward in his seat, and paid attention for the entire performance. Others have told me that although they know the history, when they experience the performance, history comes alive for them. Storytelling brings stories to life.

"Heroes" is the 100th Battalion/442nd RCT story told from the viewpoint of the Japanese Americans from Hawaii. The story follows two brothers who join the 442nd in 1943. There is friction between the Buttaheads (the Hawaii Japanese Americans) and the Kotonks (mainland Japanese Americans) until the Buttaheads visit an internment camp and realize what happened to the Kotonks. Few in Hawaii knew of the mass forced evacuations and the internment camps on the mainland. The factions unite and the 442nd is sent to Europe to fight and eventually saves the "Lost Battalion" in the Vosges Mountains in France. In the battle, one brother dies. Years after the end of the war, the surviving brother finally comes to terms with his brother's death.

In this story we see the internment through the eyes of interested outsiders. We experience a little of what it is like to go into combat for the first time and the horror of war. We gain insights into the concepts of honor and shame which drove these young men on to accomplish great feasts of heroism and sacrifice, that they might be considered average and worthy to live in the country of their birth. We are a nation of immigrants and the story of these young men striving for acceptance and respect resonates with a generation of our families at some point in time.

In times of fear and uncertainty, we will do anything to feel safe and in control. Japanese Americans commemorate the Day of Remembrance as a reminder that the needs of the state must always be balanced with the rights the citizens.

Questions for Discussion

- You have to move out of your house in two weeks and can only take one suit case weighing 50 pounds. You will be gone for an unknown period of time and there are no stores where you are going. There is no Internet or phone or cable service. What will you take with you?
- The internment camps were surrounded by guard towers, barbed wire fences, and soldiers with rifles. Do you think such measures were necessary? Why were they implemented? How would you feel if you had to live under those conditions?
- Meals in the camps were served in large mess halls like the cafeteria in your school. What would be the advantages and disadvantages of serving meals in this way? How would you feel about eating in a cafeteria for all of your meals for the next year?
- You are assigned to live in a small room with your bed a couple feet from another person who is a stranger your age. You have just enough space for your bed and frame. What adjustments will you have to make to get along in this new living space?
- If you were a Japanese American and were sent to the camps, would you have volunteered to fight for the U.S.? Would you have declined? Would you serve, if drafted? Would you have remained loyal to the USA or would you have left the country?

- The 100th Battalion/442nd RCT is the most decorated unit in U.S. military history, earning 21 Congressional Medals of Honor, 32 Distinguished Service Crosses, 560 Silver Stars, 4,000 Bronze Stars, and almost 10,000 Purple Hearts. Why do you think these Japanese Americans fought so bravely for the United States?
- There have been many times in American history when fear has led to persecution of "the other." How were the Native Americans treated during the period of Westward expansion? How did the armies of the North and South behave when invading enemy territory during the American Civil War? What happened to suspected Communist sympathizers during the McCarthy Era and the Cold War? What happened to Muslim and Arab Americans just after 9/11? What are you most afraid of now? What do you do to feel safe? What is our country doing to help you feel safe? Is it working?

Activity: I Am an American

Imagine that you are all Japanese Americans living on the West Coast in 1941 and you are keeping a diary. Please describe in your diary how you feel when you first hear about the attack on Pearl Harbor, Hawaii. How do you feel when you read the newspaper and hear people say that people like you need to be removed from your homes for the safety of the country? Describe how you feel about having to be home by the 8 pm curfew. What do you feel when you see the evacuation orders posted? What are your feelings when you first pass through the gates and barbed wire of your new home? How do you feel about being asked to volunteer to fight for the country which has incarcerated you?

The Editor

You are a newspaper editor and are writing an article for the Day of Remembrance. Has the local community ever treated a group of people or an individual unfairly out of fear or ignorance? What are the facts of the incident? How might the unfair treatment be resolved? What are the barriers to healing this situation? Should anything be done for those who were mistreated? What might be done that this type of mistreatment never happens again? What call to action would you ask your readers to undertake as individuals and as a community? Share your article and discuss.

ASSESSMENT

Students can be assessed on their participation in the discussion, and their efforts to articulate their sensitivity towards issues of victimization either during discussion or in their journal entries and "newspaper articles."

RESOURCES

Abe, Frank. *Conscience and the Constitution.* DVD. Hohokus, NJ: Transit Media, 2000.

Chung, Alton W. *Heroes.* DVD. Alton Chung, 2007.

Chung, Alton W. *Kodomo No Tame Ni (For the Sake of the Children).* CD. Alton Chung, TBD.

Ford, Jamie. *Hotel on the Corner of Bitter and Sweet: a Novel.* New York: Ballantine Books, 2009.

Fournier, Eric Paul. *Of Civil Wrongs and Rights: the Fred Korematsu Story.* San Francisco, CA: NAATA, 2000.

Horsting, Robert. *Citizen Tanouye.* DVD. WGBH Boston, MA: Boston Video, 2008.

Houston, Jeanne Wakatsuki. *Farewell to Manzanar : a True Story of Japanese American Experience During and After the World War II Internment.* Boston, MA: Houghton Mifflin, 1973.

Kessler, Lauren. *Stubborn Twig: Three Generations in the Life of a Japanese American Family.* Corvallis, OR: Oregon State University Press, 2008.

Kubota, Bill. *Most Honorable Son.* DVD. PBS Home Video, 2007.

Tanaka, Chester. *Go for Broke: A Pictorial History of the Japanese American 100th Infantry Battalion and the 442nd Regimental Combat Team.* Novato, CA: Presidio, 1997.

Weglyn, Michi. *Years of Infamy: the Untold Story of America's Concentration Camps.* Seattle, WA: University of Washington Press, 1996.

Websites

- www.densho.org On-Line Research Repository for Oral History Interviews of Japanese American Veterans and Photos from WWII
- www.goforbroke.org 100th Battalion/442nd Regimental Combat Team Educational Foundation
- www.janm.org Japanese American National Museum
- www.nisei.hawaii.edu 100th Battalion/442nd Regimental Combat Team Hawaii Veterans

Interactive Oral Histories

- www.nps.gov/manz/index.htm National Park Service Manzanar National Historic Site
- www.nps.gov/miin/index.htm National Park Service Minidoka National Historic Site
- www.cr.nps.gov/history/online_books/anthropology74/index.htm Confinement and Ethnicity: An Overview of World War II Japanese American Relocation Sites
- www.americanhistory.si.edu/perfectunion/experience/index.html Smithsonian National Museum of American History Japanese American WWII Experience
- www.pbs.org/itvs/conscience Conscience and the Constitution website: Frank Emi Story
- www.pbs.org/mosthonorableson Most Honorable Son website: Ben Kuroki Story

*Storyteller **ALTON CHUNG** combines a rich cultural heritage, drawing inspiration from his Japanese and Korean roots, as well as being influenced by the superstitions, stories, and magic of the Hawaiian Islands, where he grew up. He enjoys weaving ethnic tales, true stories, and legends from many lands, but his true passion is telling ghost stories. Learn more at www.altonchung.com.*

A Trip to Ellis Island

Donna Washington

Many elementary students are unable to imagine a life other than the one they live. They cannot conceive of a time or place that is too far outside their understanding of the world. This disbelief extends not just to time periods from hundreds of years ago, but across cultures. Students stare in wonder, confusion and sometimes suspicion at people who have 'different' clothes, habits, skin colors, priorities and beliefs. This can make it difficult for a student to connect with the very humane elements of another culture or time period.

The use of storytelling in social studies is a valuable tool in our quest to teach about the past and present in a way that doesn't gloss over the truth while explaining why things happen the way they do. Actions in context don't make them better or nobler, just less mystifying. The Ellis Island Activity is a small step towards looking at some of the forces that shaped our country.

These exercises can be done on consecutive days or accomplished over the course of a unit about immigrants who came to America through Ellis Island.

MATERIALS *for All Four Lessons*

- blank journal for each student

Lesson 1: Where Is Your Home?

OBJECTIVES *for Grade Four Residency*

Students will

- work in small cooperative groups.
- create the outline of an imaginary country.
- fill in the outline of their imaginary country.
- create a legend on their map.

- create a scale bar to indicate miles or kilometers on their map.
- write at least one paragraph as a character from their country.
- learn vocabulary: Legend, Scale Bar, Cartography, Cartographer, Anachronism.

MATERIALS

- 8½" X 11" white paper for each student
- 18" X 24" poster board for each group
- colored pencils or crayons
- rulers
- pencils
- journals

INSTRUCTIONAL PLAN

DISCUSSION **Anachronisms.** Ellis Island was in operation between 1897 and 1954. What sorts of technology did people have? Televisions? Radios? Cars? If yes, what type of cars? Trains? Electricity? Microwaves? Computers? Cell Phones? Students should be on alert for anachronisms during this exercise.

ACTIVITY 1 **Map Making.** In small groups, students should create the outline of an imaginary country on notebook paper. Each student should have a chance to draw a little bit of the outline. When they are finished it should be transferred to the poster board.

ACTIVITY 2 **Topography.** Put geographical markers on your map. Mountains, rivers, plains, and create a legend to explain the markers used. Figure out how large the country is and add a scale bar and compass.

ACTIVITY 3 **Characters.** Based on the conversation about anachronisms, students should decide who they are in this new country. What do they do and where do they live? Be certain they have chosen an appropriate job.

ACTIVITY 4 **Journaling.** Students should journal about their life in their home country.

ASSESSMENT

BASIC EVALUATION Can the student articulate the definitions of the vocabulary words? Did the student create a map with the appropriate elements? Did the student create an economy—industry, agriculture, service industry? Did the student create a persona? Did the student make a small scale map of their country? Can the student give an example of an anachronism?

EXTRA EVALUATION Can the student pass a test on the vocabulary words? Can the student identify the scale bar and legend on a map? Can the student use a legend? Can the student fill in a blank map and create a legend? Can the student calculate the distance between points using the scale bar on a map?

Lesson 2: Things Fall Apart

OBJECTIVES *for Grade Four*

Students will

- work in small groups
- employ Plan and Practice
- create three tableaux
- learn vocabulary: Tableau(x)

MATERIALS

- pencils
- writing paper

INSTRUCTIONAL PLAN

DISCUSSION Why would people leave their home countries? Discuss as many reasons as students can imagine.

CREATING TABLEAUX Tableaux are living photographs. Students should consider the placement of their bodies, limbs, and facial expressions. I usually demonstrate a tableau entitled: "OUCH! That was my foot!" I hold my foot looking pained as one student pretends she just dropped something on me. The other student points at my foot and looks very shocked. I say, "One, Two, Three Freeze!" And the three of us stand frozen in our picture.

ACTIVITY 1 **What happened.** Students decide what catastrophe or series of catastrophes struck their homeland. Only war must be unanimous.

ACTIVITY 2 **Creating Tableaux.** Plan and Practice means students sit down and plan their tableau then stand and practice their ideas.

1. The first tableau should depict a scene from the beginning of the crisis. Do we see a family arguing? A town meeting where people are scared? Plan the picture.
2. Students will speak and act respectfully to each member of the group; 'stupid' and 'no' are not allowable responses to someone's idea!
3. After planning, students stand, get in the positions they discussed and freeze for a moment to practice. No props…just imaginations. Then, they sit and plan the second picture and after practice, the third. The second tableau occurs during the height of the action. What is happening?
4. The third tableau shows us the moment when the characters decide they must leave the country and go to America.
5. When all the groups are finished. Each group shows their three pictures so we can see the progression of their problem. The teacher leads the discussion about the pictures and gives encouraging feedback.

ACTIVITY 3 **Journaling.** Students may journal about anything that happened to them while the country was in turmoil. How do they feel? Scared? Mad? Hopeful? Do they want to go to America or are they being forced?

ASSESSMENTS

BASIC EVALUATION Can students articulate the definition of the word tableau? Did the students show a progression in their images? Did students settle their disputes during planning time? Did students use their practice time effectively as they moved through the exercise? Did students participate?

EXTRA EVALUATION How involved were the student's problems? Did the group show a cohesive picture? Did each student reflect emotion on his face? Can the student spell tableau(x)?

Lesson 3: The Crossing

OBJECTIVES *for Grade Four*

Students will

- work cooperatively in small groups.
- create tableaux.

INSTRUCTIONAL PLAN

DISCUSSION What difficulties did immigrants overcome to arrive in America? What was it like on the old steamers? What did they think about America?

ACTIVITY 1 **Tableaux.** Students create four tableaux. One is of their last look at their old country. One is of something that happened while they were on board the ship. The third tableau is of something sad that occurred on the boat. The last tableau is their first sight of the Statue of Liberty.

ACTIVITY 2 **Journaling.** Students journal about their persona's journey to the U.S. Write about feelings or something left behind, or perhaps one of the events on board the ship. They should end with a statement about their expectations for the kind of life they will have here in America.

ASSESSMENTS

- Are students better at listening to each other?
- Are students more proficient at creating tableaux?
- Are students connecting the exercises with their persona?
- Are students able to articulate the conditions in steerage?

Lesson 4: A Day at Ellis Island

OBJECTIVES FOR GRADE FOUR

Students will

- articulate the process of arriving at Ellis Island.
- reflect on the hopefulness of those immigrating to America.

INSTRUCTIONAL PLAN

DISCUSSION At Ellis Island immigrants were registered, given a medical evaluation, and either quarantined, sent someplace in America as a worker, or sent to family members. A small number of people who went through Ellis Island were sent back to their home countries because they were sick or disabled. Many languages were spoken at Ellis Island and immigrants couldn't always understand the travelers around them or the Americans who were trying to register them.

ACTIVITY 1 **Arrival.** Students may only speak English to the people who were in their original country groups. To everyone else they must speak gibberish. There should be three stations set up in the room. The first station is to get registered and get a card with a number on it. The next station is the doctor. The last station is where you find out if you are quarantined, being returned to your country or being sent to the American main land.

ACTIVITY 2 **Checking In.** Students wait in line to be registered. When they tell you their name, Americanize it, and give them a card with their new name and a number on it. Next, go to the Doctor. The Doctor will put a blue mark on your card if you need to be quarantined and a red mark on your card if you are going to be sent home. Your card is unmarked if you are continuing on into America.

ACTIVITY 3 **Journaling.** Students write about the experience of their persona at Ellis Island

ASSESSMENT

The final project for this residency can be a mixed media event. Take photos of tableaux. Make videos of the students in character. Interview them at Ellis Island about how they feel about what is happening to them. Display their country maps, pictures, video and entries from their journals.

DONNA L. WASHINGTON is a published author, artist teacher and professional storyteller who started her career in 1989 after graduating from Northwestern University. She has performed and taught all over the world. Donna also has seven multiple-award winning CDs. Her publishing credits include: ***The Story of Kwanzaa, A Pride of African Tales*** *and* ***Li'l Rabbit's Kwanzaa*** *published by HarperCollins Children's Books, and* ***A Big Spooky House*** *published by Hyperion Books for Children. She lives in Durham, North Carolina with her husband and manager David, their children Devin and Darith, and their two mischievous cats Love Bug and Flash. www.Storyteller.com*

Famous Americans Wax Museum

Katie Allen, Megan Geraghty and Kristin Pilliod

OBJECTIVES *for Grades Two and Three*

Students will

- gain an appreciation of America's history by researching a famous American and how he/she contributed to our country.
- use storytelling to teach others about the life of the famous American that he/she selected to learn about.

MATERIALS

- a collection of children's biographies of famous Americans, leveled text

INSTRUCTIONAL PLAN

Students select a famous American to learn about from a classroom tub of children's biographies. Each student will spend the next few days reading and researching about the famous American he/she selected. Some questions we use to guide the students' thinking are:

- How did your famous American contribute to our country?
- What quality does your famous American model that demonstrates good citizenship?
- Why do you think this person is considered to be an American hero?
- After the students have immersed themselves in reading about their famous American, we ask them to imagine themselves as their American hero. They will write a short paragraph in character, from their famous American's point of view. The students will use storytelling to make their famous Americans come to life and teach others about their hero's contributions to America.

Over the next few days students will take on the role of a storyteller. They will think about the clothing, actions, voice, and props that will best represent their famous American and the time period he/she lived in, producing a speech, such as,

"Hello, I'm Martin Luther King Jr. I grew up in Atlanta, Georgia. At that time many laws were unfair. I couldn't go to the same schools, restaurants and even movie theatres as the white children in my community. When I grew up I traveled around the country giving speeches to try and change the unfair laws. My dream was that everyone would be treated fairly, not judged by the color of their skin."

On the day of the wax museum other classes, teachers, and parents are invited to experience a living timeline of American heroes. Each student stands frozen in character and costume, wearing a dot sticker on his/her hand. As "museum visitors," travel throughout the room, they will press each student's sticker to make him/her spring to life. The student will tell his or her famous American's story one time and then become frozen again like a wax figure until the next guest pushes his/her dot sticker.

Our wax museum lasts approximately forty five minutes. Each of the students is allowed to take a short break and travel throughout the room to learn about other famous American heroes from their peers.

WAX MUSEUM *(left photo) Barack Obama (alias Steven Gurthy), Walt Disney (alias Joyce Hsieh), Pocahontas (alias Allison Hinden). (right photo) Abe (alias Ryan Gibbs, JFK (alias Ethan Golde), MLK, Jr. (alias R.J. Gorczyca)*

ASSESSMENT

Assessment data can be collected over the course of the project. Teachers may use observation, student writing and storytelling presentation to measure each student's understanding.

The wax museum is easily adapted to meet the needs of all learners. The reading level of the children's biographies, length of written work and storytelling presentation can be modified to meet individual student needs. Visual, auditory, and kinesthetic learners will all benefit from this learning experience. We found our students were highly motivated and actively engaged throughout the course of this project. To this day former students still reflect on the fun they had and the learning they experienced participating in the "Second Grade Famous American Wax Museum."

MEGAN GERAGHTY, *Katie Allen, and Kristin Pilliod are second grade teachers at Claymont Elementary in the Parkway School District, MO. Megan has a B.A. in early childhood education from St. Louis University, an M.A. in elementary education from Lindenwood University, and has completed 30 additional graduate hours in the field of education. Megan has been teaching for 23 years and has taught kindergarten, second and third grades.*

KATIE ALLEN *has a B.A. in Elementary Education and an M.A. in Curriculum and Instruction from the University of Missouri-Columbia. She has completed an additional thirty graduate hours in the field of education. This is her twelfth year teaching in the Parkway School District, MO. She has taught both first and second grade students.*

KRISTIN PILLIOD *has a B.A. in Early Childhood Education from the University of Missouri-Columbia and a M.A. in Special Reading from Lindenwood University. This is her sixth year teaching in the Parkway School District, MO. She has taught both kindergarten and second grade students.*

Curious About the World

BUILDING A CULTURE OF INQUIRY THROUGH ORAL HISTORY

Jo Radner

"Young children are researchers. It's their way of life."
PAULA ROGOVIN

OBJECTIVES

Students will

- develop research projects and interview family and community members either individually, in teams, or as a whole class.
- come to understand and appreciate the lives and legacies of people in previous generations, the diverse cultures within their own community, and their own place in history.

MATERIALS

If students are to record interviews, a simple digital audio recorder (also, preferably, an external microphone) with the ability to download to computers is needed.

The Projects

"We want our students to know that history is stories about the past," the principal said to me. "Can you help us?" The phone call triggered a year's residency in a third-to-fifth grade school. The students learned to see themselves as researchers as they interviewed and collected stories from older people in their community.

The Town before the Fire

Fire Story Quilt

Each class developed its own project.

- Focusing on a traumatic local event, the 1947 wildfire that destroyed 80% of the buildings in the town, the third grade researched photos, visited the local historical society museum, interviewed residents who had experienced the fire, and created a scale model of the town center as it had been before the fire.
- One fourth grade class interviewed family members and neighbors about the fire and created a story quilt of drawings and personal responses to what they heard.
- Another fourth grade class interviewed one older resident and wrote individual biographies that reflected their different interests in the stories she told.
- Some fourth and fifth grade students interviewed older family members about various life experiences, including their military service in World War II, Korea, and Vietnam, and then transcribed the results to write reports.

Reaching out more widely into the community, fourth and fifth graders transformed the school's traditional March Spaghetti Supper into a public evening of story-gathering and storytelling.

- A week before the event, a press release in the local paper invited older residents to the supper. A curious crowd turned out in record numbers.
- Student "Story Ambassadors" greeted adults at the door and invited them to wear "I have a story to tell" buttons.

- Laminated placemats prompted suppertime conversations ("How did you get your first job?" "What is your favorite memory from school?").
- As diners finished their meals, the ambassadors, cruising the cafeteria escorted button-wearers to the school library, where classmates were staffing two interview areas with recorders, release forms, and eager listeners.
- The resultant interviews were archived in the local historical society so that other researchers could use them—a rare achievement for elementary students.

All students found significant roles in these projects. Shy students or those with behavior disabilities often teamed up with interviewers to run recorders or take photos, and later contributed to reports. Students with limited writing abilities illustrated stories and dictated observations to team members. One French-speaking student interviewed her grandmother and translated the story of her immigration from Quebec.

At the close of the year, many positive results were reported.

- Students whose family members had been interviewed felt proud and gained new insight into their own history.
- Teachers new to the district felt more at home.
- Community members came in greater numbers to volunteer at the school.
- Pointing with pride to buildings and people in town, students told the stories they had heard.

A new web of friendship and appreciation had grown.

CLASS ORAL HISTORY PROJECTS – POTENTIAL OUTCOMES

Exhibits
Board games
Web sites
Radio programs
Readers' theater
Walking tours
Maps and scale models
Biographies
Brochures
Story quilts, murals
Community heritage events
Newscasts
School/town story day
Paintings, collages, drawings
Historical drama
Poetry, stories
Archival deposits

INSTRUCTIONAL PLAN

Oral history programs can contribute to myriad projects. All have the great virtue that students see themselves as explorers and creators, actively engaging with families and communities for the public benefit. And all projects, no matter what their outcomes, require students to develop good interviewing skills. The better the interview, the better the story.

How does an interviewer invite good stories? They invite good stories by first learning enough about the topic and the teller (the interviewee) to understand what is being discussed and to predict fruitful lines of inquiry. Then by starting conversations with open-ended questions, listening carefully to the responses, and developing prompts for more details and explanation. Essential elementary skills are involved:

- reading for information
- predicting and developing topics for investigation
- asking questions
- listening with comprehension
- analyzing responses
- asking follow-up questions for understanding.

Engaged wholeheartedly in the process, students gladly work on those skills. Gathering oral history is like a treasure hunt.

I find the following class interviewing exercises useful from third grade through high school. (For younger students, see the excellent ideas in Rogovin 1998.)

MODEL INTERVIEW 1:
The limits of closed/fact-seeking questions; introducing open-ended questioning.

The teacher and another adult model an interview, one as interviewer, the other as teller, on a simple topic (for instance, games played in childhood, or the teller's favorite teacher in elementary school). The interviewer should ask only closed questions (questions that can be answered with "yes" or "no" or a fact), and the teller should answer with only the minimum information the question requires. Avoid open-ended follow-up questions.

"Who was your favorite teacher when you were in school?"
Mrs. Green.

"Did she read to you?"
Yes.

"What grade did she teach?"
Third.

And so on.

Stop the interview and ask the class, "Is this an interesting interview?" When they say no (and they will, if you've made it boring enough), ask, "What would you like to hear about Mrs. Green that would be interesting?" After several suggestions, ask, "How could the interviewer phrase a question that would invite that kind of information/story?" Take some ideas, working towards introducing the idea of open-ended questions: questions that invite long, detailed answers, in contrast to closed questions. You might share a list of open-ended question beginnings (examples shown at right).

Brainstorm a list of open-ended questions the interviewer could ask the interviewee about "Mrs. Green," write them on the board, then try out a few of them with the teller to demonstrate the way they call forth stories. Discuss why these answers are more interesting.

SOME WAYS TO BEGIN OPEN-ENDED QUESTIONS:

Tell me about...
What was it like to...
Can you describe...
Why...
How...
Describe a typical day in your life when you were...
Tell me about the first time you...
Can you give me an example of...
Can you tell me about your biggest success at...

MODEL INTERVIEW 2: *Starter questions and follow-up*

To prepare to do an interview, students need to decide what kinds of things they want to learn—in the process, predicting what they think the teller will be able to talk about. In advance of the second model interview, select another topic and ask the students to brainstorm open-ended questions that could be asked of the teller. Write the questions on the board, reinforcing the concept of open-ended structure; then have the class choose two or three different questions to be asked during the interview.

Once you have this final list, stress to the students that these are "*starter* questions"—that is, each one is just the beginning of a conversation. Tell the class that the teacher/interviewer will ask a starter question, then the students will listen to the answer and think of *follow-up* questions that will help them learn more about the topic. Most follow-up questions should also be open-ended, though it is fine to ask for a few facts, too.

Then the teacher and another adult will begin the model interview with one of the chosen starter questions. The teller should answer with a few details, but should leave some things sketchy or create dangling hints to suggest follow-up.

Teacher: *"Please tell me about your favorite games when you were in [fourth] grade."*

[Teller lists a few games he/she liked, mentioning some game the current students don't play—mumblety-peg? marbles? kick the can?]

Teacher to class: "What would you like to learn more about? What might we ask in order to understand *X* better? to learn more of the story?"

The class brainstorms follow-up questions, again guided to think about open-ended questioning. (Sometimes it works best to ask students to share ideas in pairs before the whole-class discussion.)

The teacher chooses one suggested follow-up question (e.g., "How did you play mumblety-peg?") and asks the teller, who provides more details. Continue this pattern through a few more follow-up questions, so that students can see how interesting it is to look for fuller stories in an interview. Once the momentum flags on the first starter question go back to the list on the board, move to the next topic, and model another round of starter and follow-up.

In this exercise, keep reminding students to listen closely to what the teller says, so that they can spot places where more details might help understanding, or where there might be more interesting stories to hear. Students can use paper and pencil during this exercise to jot down words (or draw pictures) to remind them of ideas for follow-up.

It's also useful to build into the exercise a few moments when the interviewer stops, asks the students, "How could you tell that I was really listening and interested in what the teller was saying?" and collects observations from students that make them more sensitive to what has been called "performing listening" (Wagler et al., p. 35). Body language, facial expression, eye contact, and gestures are all important interviewing tools.

MODEL INTERVIEW 3:
From Research to Interview: The Class Interview

Depending on the class's project, this exercise will be either a warm-up for team or home family interviews or—if you plan a series of classroom interviews—the first step in your actual project. I have found that for third graders and some fourth graders, oral history interviewing is most successful in the classroom, with tellers visiting for 30-45 minutes and the teacher processing the visit with the students immediately afterwards. More mature fourth and fifth graders can interview in pairs outside the classroom, and most students can successfully interview family members on their own.

For this exercise, invite a class parent or grandparent or a genial community member to be the "model teller." (Alternatively, I have performed this exercise quite successfully by asking another adult to be the teller but to pretend to be his/her own grandparent. Students cheerfully go along with the pretense as long as the teller stays in historical character.) Explain in advance to the teller that because the class is just beginning to learn interviewing skills, the teacher will stop the interview occasionally for side-coaching.

A few days before the interview takes place, share with the class some facts about the teller: name, birth date, some biographical details. Choose one or two relevant events during the teller's life for the class to research (military service? civil rights movement? nuclear accident at Three Mile Island? women's liberation?), or focus on the teller's occupation or expertise. Students research the topic, then brainstorm starter questions based on what they have learned from their research and what they predict the teller might have experienced. After the class has selected starter questions and you have reminded them about the importance of follow-up, bring the teller to the class for the interview. This time the students, not the teacher, will ask the questions, raising their hands so that the teacher can call on them.

Since this is the last model interview exercise, build into it some practice in recording and/or taking notes on what the teller says, and on writing up the results after the interview. Students unable to write notes may draw pictures to remind themselves of important points. With a young class, stop the interview from time to time to check understanding, review what has been said, and allow (and teach) note-taking. (For a fine example of an interviewing and note-taking program in a first-grade class, see Rogovin 1998.)

It is important to pause several times during this interview, not only to coach the students on effective questioning and follow-up, but also to point out what they are doing right: performing listening, paying attention to answers, asking open-ended questions, following up. This is a good opportunity to point out how their research has made them more competent and confident interviewers.

If you record the interview, later you can play back selected moments and debrief with students about what was happening. For transcription practice, assign students short sections of the recording to transcribe, check, revise, and print.

ASSESSMENT

Oral history projects ask students to do authentic tasks beyond their usual sphere (even if interviews are limited to the classroom) and to produce potentially public results. Observation of all stages of this process is part of assessment. A few questions: Can students perform background research and shape their new knowledge into open-ended questions that relate to tellers' lives? Can they focus on the answers and ask follow-up questions that extend their understanding? Do their final projects show new awareness of the world beyond the school and their relationship to it?

RELATED RESOURCES

Books

- Ritchie, Donald. *Doing Oral History.* Twayne's Oral History Series, Vol. 15. New York, NY: Twayne Publishers, 1995. A comprehensive guide for oral historians of all levels of expertise. Not aimed at school projects, but a useful handbook.
- Rogovin, Paula. *Classroom Interviews: A World of Learning.* Portsmouth, NH: Heinemann, 1998. This book shows how to plan a curriculum for first grade children based on classroom interviewing of family and community members, relevant to social studies, writing, reading, science, and math.
- Winston, Linda. *Keepsakes: Using Family Stories in Elementary Classrooms.* Portsmouth, NH: Heinemann, 1997. Excellent accounts of multicultural family-interviewing projects and curricula in elementary grades. This is a comprehensive annotated bibliography of picture books on family history.

Websites

- Chace, Karen. "Oral History Resources." http://www.storybug.net/links/oralhistory.html superb collection of online resources for teachers, including guides, lesson plans, and examples.
- Montana Heritage Project. http://www.montanaheritageproject.org/ A model intergenerational oral history project, conducted by teachers dedicated to training young people to think deeply about the world they face and their community's place in it.
- StoryCorps Question Generator. http://storycorps.org/record-your-story/question-generator/list/ Marvelous suggestions for developing questions on family history.
- Veterans History Project. http://www.loc.gov/vets/. American Folklife Center, Library of Congress. Collected histories from veterans, how-to instructions for interviewers, excellent suggestions for interview questions about wartime matters.
- Wagler, Mark, Ruth Olson, and Anne Pryor. "Kids' Guide to Local Culture." Madison, WI: Madison Children's Museum, 2004. http://csumc.wisc.edu/cmct/HmongTour/howwedidit/LOCAL_KIDS_GUIDE_WEB.pdf Written for students, with useful hints about interviewing, about observing culture, about identifying meaningful folklore in family and community.

*Folklorist, storyteller, writer, and oral historian, **JO RADNER** creates personal tales and stories about the people and history of northern New England. She performs at theaters, festivals, conferences, schools, and community events, and has taught classes and workshops in storytelling and oral history for more than 30 years. Past president of the American Folklore Society, Washington Storytellers Theatre, and the National Storytelling Network, she serves on the Advisory Board of Storytelling, Self, Society: An Interdisciplinary Journal of Storytelling Studies. She is Adjunct Professor at Lesley University and Professor Emerita from American University in Washington, DC. www.joradner.com.*

Asase Ye Duru: "The Earth has Weight"

Proverb: tumi nyina ne asase:

"All power emanates from the earth."

This symbol represents earth's divinity,

providence, power, wealth.

CHAPTER THREE

National Council of Social Studies 3. People, Places & Environments

Social studies programs should include experiences that provide for the study of people, places, and environments.

The study of people, places, and environments enables us to understand the relationship between human populations and the physical world.

Learners develop an understanding of spatial perspectives, and examine changes in the relationship between peoples, places and environments.

Today's social, cultural, economic and civic issues demand that students apply as they knowledge, skills, and understandings as they address questions such as: *Why do people decide to live where they do or move to other places?* ■ *Why is location important?* ■ *How do people interact with the environment and what are some of the consequences of those interactions?* ■ *What physical and other characteristics lead to the creation of regions?* ■ *How do maps, globes, geographic tools and geospatial technologies contribute to the understanding of people, places, and environments?*

In schools this theme typically appears in units and courses dealing with geography, regional studies, and world cultures.

CAROL BIRCH | KATHLEEN McKAY McKENNA
BRANDI SELF | JANE STENSON | AYA BORCHERS

On Setting

Carol Birch

"If you don't know where you are,
you don't know who you are."
WENDELL BERRY

One of the great paradoxes of stories is how completely they stir us with the universality of the human heart, while they simultaneously honor and accentuate what is specific and unique to a culture. Today, as I wilt on a sweltering day in July, a friend sends an email from "wintry Namibia." I forget winter's bite when limp from humidity. My friend's email reminds me not only of how varied the world actually is, but also how easily I fall back into believing that my reality of "July" is everyone's reality of July's weather.

One of my favorite books, *On the Same Day in March: A Tour of the World's Weather* by Marilyn Singer (Harpercollins, 2000), shows how radically different weather conditions effect lives in seventeen locations around the world. Singer's concrete verbs, deft descriptions and refrain "On the same day in March" offer a vibrant and celebratory experience of the world through its weather. She includes the contrasts of freezing "floes of ice" in the Arctic, "the sun's shy smile" in Paris and moves on to the heat of central Thailand. As a few uniformed children stand at a blackboard in an open air classroom in Thailand, we read: "It's too hot to plant rice. It's too hot to pick rice. But it's not too hot to spell R I C E..." Singer, along with lively illustrations by Frane Lessac, reminds us that fog is not one experience; fog can delicately thread through temples in the Nile Valley or settle heavily on a swamp in a Louisiana bayou. As she highlights the weather, she also draws attention to the setting's options for work and for play. Adults and children gather at a busy market place in Dakar, Senegal, load a boat on the Amazon River in Brazil and work on ranches in both the Texas Panhandle and Patagonia, Argentina. They play basketball in the school yard in New York City, picnic in a park in Xian, China; hit a ball on a beach in Barbados or splash in the river in northern Kenya. Singer touches on the universal appeal of longing for change in the weather when people feel oppressed by days that are too hot, too cold or too grey for too long. This book implicitly revels in all peoples of the earth, as it explicitly demonstrates that where people live inextricably influences how they live.

I would go so far as to say where and when we live functions in our lives as the warp, the threads that stretch lengthwise on the loom of life; how we live—what we do within those givens—is the weft, the crosswise threads woven under and over the warp to make fabric. When we are young, it is unusual to be conscious of how the physical features of where we live frame our lives. It's as much a given as the air we breathe. But, as storytellers, we have to become more aware first of the frames that limit our point of view and then the unconscious assumptions beneath the framework.

For the last thirty years I've used a series of questions to explore and develop setting in stories. Initially I used them in my own preparation of stories, and then in workshops, recording them on a cassette and finally publishing them in *The Whole Story Handbook: Using Imagery to Complete the Story Experience* (August House, 2000). One goal was to make a story more compelling by moving it from merely an intellectual exercise into a fuller sensory/kinetic approach. A second goal was to make it more real, so that storytellers speak with perceivable attitudes about the people, places and events within the stories from printed sources, as they do when speaking to friends about their lives. The questions were an invitation to fall into a sensual reverie. Now I challenge you to first answer those questions about your own world, or, if you work with children, to have them look at their world in very specific ways. We cannot effectively build bridges between cultures without a firm footing in our own culture. If we lack awareness of, or if we lack a vocabulary to describe the world we live in, how can we paint pictures of worlds we imagine? This is an invitation to wake up to our own landscapes before turning the questions to the setting of a story.

Consider where you physically live: continent, country, region, community, home:

- What effects do season, climate and weather have on your life?
- How many seasons does your year usually have?
- How many climates do you live in?
- On a particular day, how are your senses stirred by weather?
    - Describe sights associated with it.
    - Listen for sounds associated with it.

  - When you inhale, are there pleasant scents or unpleasant smells?
  - What particular tastes are associated with it?
  - How does the weather feel on your skin?
- What feelings does the weather arouse in you?

Author and storyteller Lynn Moroney, who lives in Oklahoma, joked that during her first visit to New England she was afraid that if she put her purse down, she might knock Rhode Island into the ocean. She lives in a region of America whose glorious landscape is based in part on the vastness of the sky. All the expansiveness of Oklahoma's horizon leaves me, a New Englander, feeling exposed and vulnerable; I contract while she luxuriates in its vast spaciousness.

- Think about the terrain around your home:
- When you go outside, what frames the horizon?
- What are the land's most distinguishing features?
- What reveals wild or civilizing influences?
- What reveals human carefulness or recklessness?
- When was the last time you touched the soil?
- Describe the soil in terms of your senses (though you may want to skip taste!).
- Is the land productive?
- What is growing? Flourishing? Languishing?
- What kind of work is possible or required near home or in the community?
- What kinds of pets are near home or in the community?
- Do any undomesticated animals live here? Are they welcomed, disliked or feared?
- What pleasurable activities fit in near home or in the community?
- Where in this outside space do you feel hidden or exposed, safe or threatened?
- What is pleasing, or not, near home or in the community?

If you cannot experience another land first hand, seek out those who lived there. A different environment requires new ways of thinking. Ask people who have moved into your area from another region or another country:

- What do they miss?
- What did they have to give up to live here?
- What were the biggest surprises of their new environment?
- What are their biggest pleasures here?

I worked in a supposedly homogeneous suburban community in Westchester, New York; in actuality a wonderful diversity of people live there. As part of a library program on a local cable station, I asked women and men to describe their experiences after school on an ordinary day in terms of their five senses. Participants chose the year of their typical day after school. Two participants were born in the USA: a man from Wisconsin whose bicycle brought a new freedom and bravado to his life, and a very urban woman who worked at Bloomingdale's department store as a teenager. The others came from a variety of nations: China, Czechoslovakia, Ethiopia/Yemen, India, Israel, Miramar and Pakistan. What did they all of them regret? That their children and/or grandchildren do not know the freedom each of them enjoyed during long hours of unsupervised play. What did they all miss? Bread! The bread of their childhoods—remembered as warmer, crustier, denser and more flavorful than the over-processed, white-bread world of the usual U.S. grocery store.

How their faces lit up as they described the bread they devoured in childhood and salivated for as adults. That internal fire lit by first-hand experience and fueled by memory is usually missing when someone learns just the words of a story. The words are there to call up tactile sensations and emotional experiences; our hearts and senses are needed to tell a story along with the attention of our minds.

Sensory impressions make a place and its stories more compelling, which is why there is no substitute for the first-hand experience of a country—its sights, sounds, tastes, textures and aromas. Travel, talking to others about their lives in other places, and reading great books can all introduce us other places or time. They can also serve as wake-up calls reminding us how much we don't know, and how much we never even knew to consider.

Landscapes function as pervasively as characters in most stories. All too often in contemporary America, "Rapunzel" is known in its Disney-fied version and dismissed merely as a "nursery tale." William Irwin Thompson in his book *Imaginary Landscape: Making Worlds of Myth and Science* (St. Martin's Press, 1989) gives a startling example of how deeply geography—in this case flora—shapes this tale. During her pregnancy, Rapunzel's mother craves rampion, an herb planted in the fall and used in winter salads. The reproductive life of this plant mirrors the plot of the story: the plant can fertilize itself as it rises like a column, splits in two and the halves curl like braids on girl's head: "So Rapunzel does indeed have a tower, does indeed send out a call for the male to come and pollinate her, and does indeed have 'collecting hairs' that allow her to draw up the male into intimate contact with her reproductive organs..." This information from a book published more than twenty-two years ago continues to be startling news to most of us.

As I wrote in *The Whole Story Handbook* (August House, 2000), storytellers need to know these basics about setting in any story they want to tell:

- "How does setting function in your story?
- What indicators of era and locale would appear in a mural of the story?
- What about this time and place binds the characters together?
- What is important historically about the time and place of the story?
- What about this time and place makes you want to return to it repeatedly?"

"If you continue to have difficulty identifying how important the setting is in the story, retell the story, changing the era and then the locale. Whatever alterations appear in the retelling indicate time and place in the original story. Look at the story and consider what remains when you remove all explicit and implicit details of locale and era. You won't see much beyond the bones of the sequence of the plot and stick figures for characters." Time and place, setting and period are that pervasive within stories.

It is the great gift of stories to build the bridges across geographic, ethnic, religious, cultural and historical divides. Stories broaden our world but we face the chicken and the egg paradox. Stories can help us become more conscious, but we also have to be more conscious when we delve into them. Let me end with a favorite metaphor. I like to think of the center of the world as a boiling broth of universality—the pain of loss, the joy of love, etc. Each place—from settlements to nations—ladles out this broth of universally shared experiences and then seasons it. Seasonings are gathered from what is at hand through their geographic, ethnic, religious, cultural and historical details to create distinct flavors. Soup's on. Dip in and savor!

RESOURCES

Birch, Carol. *The Whole Story Handbook: Using Imagery to Complete the Story Experience.* Little Rock: August House, 2000.

Thompson, Irwin. *Imaginary Landscape: Making Worlds of Myth and Science.* New York: St. Martin's Press, 1989.

CAROL BIRCH *received the Circle of Excellence, an award given by peers to storytellers honored as masters who set the standards for excellence. All of her books and recordings received a variety of awards from the American Library Association, Parent's Choice, NAPPA (National Parenting Publications), the Anne Izard Storytellers' Choice and Storytelling World. As teller and teacher she's performed at the National Storytelling Festival in Jonesborough, TN, as well as at regional festivals, conferences, and universities nationwide. Media appearances include ABC's Nightline, CBS' Morning Show and National Public Radio. Her stories bring to life legendary Americans like Lou Gehrig, as well as the unheralded in words of renowned authors like John Steinbeck and Ray Bradbury. Birch's storytelling is like "a very dry martini - smooth, intoxicating and little dangerous." www.carolbirchstoryteller.com*

Telling Our Own Stories in the Middle School Social Studies Classroom

Kathleen McKay McKenna

OBJECTIVES *for Middle School*

Students will

- understand the relationships between human populations and the physical world and examine changes in the relationships between peoples, places, and environments.
- develop an understanding of spatial perspectives.
- apply knowledge, skills and understandings as they address such questions as
- why do people decide to live where they do or move to other places?
- why is location important?
- how do people interact with the environment and what are some consequences of those interactions?
- what physical and other characteristics lead to the creation of regions?
- how do maps, globes, geographic tools and geospatial technologies contribute to the understanding of people, places, and environments?

MATERIALS

Students need supplies to create "visuals."

- in class—construction paper, paint, scissors, glue, markers for presentation board
- from home—bring in pictures of trips or artifacts that support their story
- teacher letter to parents explaining the family history project and obtaining permission to bring family artifacts to school

ORIGINS OF THE STORY

As a social studies teacher who had hated the dry, dull years of middle school, high school and college history classes wherein I was forced to memorize battles, generals, and dates, but who loves maps, faraway places, and geography concepts in general, I made up my mind early on in my career that my classroom would involve more hands-on, active and personal learning than rote, seat learning from a textbook. Because I had been lucky enough to work on the geography standards with the Illinois Council for the Social Studies, I was steeped in the power of those ideas to help students learn history and geography together as critically interconnected parts of the same story.

Accordingly, I decided that I could help my students, whom I taught through sixth, seventh and eighth grades, increase their higher order thinking skills if I were to teach them the five themes of geography in the beginning of sixth grade and have them make connections to those throughout their remaining years with me (and hopefully, if it worked, to continue to use the concepts well beyond middle school). The first two geography themes, location and place, are fairly straightforward and easy to discover as factual information, the last three require some research and far more sophisticated thinking skills to understand well and be able to apply.

LOCATION—absolute (latitude and longitude) and/or relative (e.g. south of Boston, west of Narragansett Bay)

PLACE—answers what the specific area is like, e.g., topography, weather, people's history and subsequent attitudes

REGION—answers what the larger region (of which the specific area is a part) is like, e.g., New England has a temperate climate, some of the oldest European history in the country, seafood industries

HUMAN AND ENVIRONMENTAL INTERACTION—how do people affect the environment (e.g., depleting or enhancing farm lands or fishing areas) and how the environment affects people (e.g., good soil for agriculture or destruction from hurricanes or other natural disasters)

MOVEMENT OF GOODS, PEOPLE AND IDEAS—why do people move, what ideas and goods do they take with them and for what purpose, and how does that movement affect them and others whom they encounter

Pondering the best way to help my students understand these ideas, I naturally thought of my own "story," i.e., how and where the five themes had affected my life. Because I grew up in Wickford, Rhode Island, a small New England town where my father was bake master for the annual clambake and where I had lived through a number of impressive hurricanes, I knew I could spin a good tale about how the environment directly impacted my young life and vice-versa. I remembered my dad telling me that the Narragansett Indians had taught the first settlers in Wickford how to dig clams and catch lobsters in traps, then prepare and eat them by steaming them over hot stones covered in seaweed. Aha, thought I: the movement of ideas from one group of people to another! I've got two of the themes covered easily.

Of course the region of New England is fairly easy to describe with its connection to the earliest European settlers, its shared history and intertwined economies, and its location on the Atlantic Ocean. Once I had the latitude and longitude of Wickford and its placement relative to the ocean to the east, Massachusetts to the north, Connecticut to the west and south, I had all the themes of geography covered in my own story.

DEVELOPMENT OF THE INSTRUCTIONAL PLAN

The first year into teaching the five big geography ideas, I simply covered them in the textbook with the kids, told my story as an example of how they existed in and affected my life, and had the students pick out the five themes in my story. But, as students who are expected and encouraged to share their ideas will do, my students immediately started to tell me stories about their families' run-ins with the weather, with things they bought on trips to other places, about people they had met who shared stories with them about their lives. One of my students asked, "So, Mrs. McKenna, do you mean, like, if we brought home some weaving from the native people in Arizona and told our friends about how we saw them doing it, that would be, like, the movement of ideas?" They got it! And I realized they could all talk about it better and "get it" more deeply by preparing and telling their stories, rather than just being the audience for mine.

The first rule of good teaching is good listening, so good teachers understand that almost all kids (except the deeply shy ones) love talking about themselves; indeed, don't we all? Accordingly, I used what they loved as a way to learn the geography themes in meaningful and long-term ways. I had them talk with their families to help create the stories, adding strong details and embellishing with anecdotes of trips or weather events, then they made index cards with notes to help them through the presentation.

Naturally, however, because props are good for stories, the kids began to bring pictures or maps or mementos to make the stories even better. I realized that they could "blow out" their stories and really show their understanding by creating any kind of visual they pleased to go with the story. One year a student brought his grandmother's samovar, which had traveled with the family from Russia during the pogroms of the early 20th century and was still used as a teapot for important family celebrations. The class then discussed the many different kinds of kitchen and dining room implements and articles that may have their origins in other cultures, even different styles of furniture. This was the kind of "small miracle" which led to connected, analytic and synthetic thinking in the classroom.

Most important, all students could do this well, especially with the rubric assessment *(see Figure 1, next page)* we created together: with a rubric that covers the geography themes, the presentation itself, the appearance of the visuals, and the creativity involved in planning and putting it all together, every child has both the ability and possibility of scoring well in one area to compensate for other weaknesses. Importantly, creating the rubric together before creating the project and going over the rubric during and after the presentation naturally allows the students to perform the critical meta-cognitive skill of determining how to use their strengths to support their weaker areas for future projects.

OUTCOME

Beyond exceeding the standards in multiple curricular areas, developing higher order thinking skills (e.g., analysis, evaluation, synthesis), working on their metacognitive strategies, and beginning to make solid connections between and among curricular areas, the best outcome of this project is how well the children listen to each other's stories and how that leads them to appreciate everyone's background and history. When we discover both how much we have in common and what is unique about us, we begin to lay the groundwork for respecting the possibilities of all people.

Figure 1: The assessment rubric

FIVE THEMES	FOUR	THREE	TWO	ONE
Presentation clearly presents: location, place, region, human and environmental interaction, and the movement of goods, people and ideas	Only four of the five themes appear in the story	Only three of the five themes appear in the story	Only two or three of the themes appear in the story	Only one of the themes appears in the story
Oral Presentation: preparation and voice	Student has polished presentation, modulates and varies voice to show meaning and emotion	Student has practiced presentation somewhat and show some ability to modulate and vary voice to show meaning and emotion	Student has only somewhat practiced presentation, and voice modulation and variety are below average	Student has not practiced presentation, nor does she modulate or vary voice so presentation is flat
Visual Aids	Student has put great energy and effort into preparing and presenting visuals that support the story	Student has put some energy and effort into preparing and presenting visuals that support the story	Student has put little energy and effort into preparing and presenting visuals that support the story	Student has put no energy or effort into preparing and presenting visuals that support the story
Creativity and Effort	Student has focused energy and effort on making presentation original and informative	Student has focused some energy and effort on making presentation mostly original and informative	Student has focused a little energy and effort on making presentation somewhat original and informative	Student has focused little to no energy or effort on making presentation original or informative
Focus during class time	Excellent and consistent	Above average and generally consistent	Only average and inconsistent	Poor and not generally consistent

***KATHLEEN MCKENNA** grew up in a family of Irish Catholic linguists/ blarney-makers and Scottish Presbyterian salesmen. Her story is woven from pieces of all their stories. Naturally, she would become a storytelling teacher... in a progressive school. Semi-retired from teaching in Chicago, she is now back in Rhode Island with her large family, all of whom love retelling the old stories as well as making new ones. You can contact her at mckk77@gmail.com*

See Rock City

Brandi Self

OBJECTIVES *for Grade Four*

Students will

- learn about the history and culture of the Nez Perce tribe.
- identify communication techniques used by the Native Americans.
- understand how storytelling helped Native Americans learn about the history and land of their people.
- identify landforms of their state and important rock formations.
- create a tale that incorporates state landforms and rock formations along with the characteristics of a trickster tale.

MATERIALS

- "Coyote and the Heart of the Monster," a Nez Perce Tale. A version of the story is included below; other versions can be found at: http://www.juntosociety.com/native/nezperce8.htm
- photos of the Heart of the Monster Landforms sihttp://www.nps.gov/nepe/naturescience/naturalfeaturesandecosystems.htm
- Rock City http://seerockcity.com/pages/ The-Geographic-Wonders-of-Rock-City

INSTRUCTIONAL PLAN

"Welcome to my fourth grade classroom. We're beginning a new social studies unit. Listen in…

"This year we have been learning about several different landmarks found in the United States. One of the landmarks we learned about was the Grand Canyon. If we wanted to drive to the Grand Canyon, how would we figure out how to get there?"

Possible student answers would include map, GPS, atlas, internet.

"You are right; all of these are resources that would help us find our destination. How would these resources help us?"

They would give us the road names we needed to travel to the Grand Canyon.

"Exactly. We use road names to help us communicate how to get from one place to another. This wasn't always the case. Long ago, before the Europeans came to North America, there weren't set roads used for travel. Why not?"

Deer trails. Cow paths. Cars had not been invented yet.

"So, if there weren't roads to help the Native Americans communicate how to get from one place to another, how do you think they did it? How were they able to remember and pass on directions for getting from one place to another?"

Students brainstorm in pairs, then pairs share with the class. I make sure they understand that landmarks were often used to describe the route/path that the group should take.

"We have studied many different Native American Tribes this year. Many of the tribes we have studied were migratory tribes. What are migratory tribes?"

Tribes that travel with the seasons and don't have one permanent home are migratory.

"Why were tribes migratory?"

They often moved with the seasons to locations that were abundant with food (animals/plants).

"One Native American group that we haven't studied about yet is the Nez Perce. The Nez Perce are a tribe that followed a predictable pattern from permanent winter villages through several temporary camps, nearly always returning to the same locations year after year. The women dug root crops in the early spring. The men caught salmon in the rivers. In the summer, they moved into mountain meadows, living in easily transported tipis, hunting and fishing and digging more roots, like the wild carrot and wild potato. Those foods, along with dried berries, nuts, and dried meat would feed the people all winter when they moved back to their snug wooden longhouses. The Nez Perce are known for many things, including helping Lewis and Clark on their expedition. They are also famous for their storytelling. They would pass down stories from generation to generation to help the tribe members understand their history and culture. They would also use stories to help communicate directions for getting from one location to another when they migrated from their summer to winter homes. They would incorporate the landforms into their stories to make them more meaningful and easy to remember.

"Early this year we discussed trickster tales. Who remembers a trickster tale that we learned about?"

Br'er Rabbit, Raven, Coyote.

"What are the characteristics of a trickster tale?"

Good vs. Evil, animals talk, teach a lesson, problem/solution.

"Most Nez Perce tales included Coyote as a trickster. Coyote was a powerful being for the Nez Perce, and because of this he often played a large role in their stories. Coyote was a teacher, trickster, or hero depending on the particular story. I want you to listen as I tell you the story 'Coyote and the Heart of the Monster.' As you listen to the story, see if you can pick up on the landforms that are mentioned or described in the story.

Coyote and the Heart of the Monster

retold by Sherry Norfolk

Coyote was building a fish ladder to help the people catch salmon when Old Woman shouted to him, "Why are you bothering with that? All of the people are gone. A Giant Monster has eaten them all!"

"Well," said Coyote to himself, "then I'll stop doing this because I was doing it for the people, and now I guess I'll have to go along and save them."

Of course, Coyote had never seen a Giant Monster—but he figured the Giant Monster couldn't be much bigger than a bull moose, and certainly Coyote could take down a moose!

Coyote packed up his bag, taking along the things he always carried: a flint fire-making kit, a bundle of dry sticks to build a fire, and five sharp knives. Coyote never went anywhere without those things.

continued

Then Coyote went along upstream, by way of the Salmon River country, until he saw the mouth of a huge cave, right in the middle of the path...Coyote went along into the cave... the path was slippery and dark, getting darker and slipperier as he went along...went along...PUM! Coyote tripped over something in the darkness!

"Ouch!" he heard a woman moan. "Oooooh, you kicked me in the ribs...."

Coyote reached into his pack and brought out the fire-making kit. He struck a flame and lit one of the sticks for a torch.

"Please forgive me, but I didn't see you in this dark cave. I'm looking for the Giant Monster. Can you help me find him?"

"Heh, heh, heh...help you find him? You're in him!"

"What are you talking about? I'm in a cave."

"You're in the belly of the Giant Monster...and so am I. It's easy to walk in, but you can never get out. The monster is so big your eyes can't take him in—his body fills the whole valley. There are many people farther along the path. And we're all starving to death. Do you have any food, Coyote?"

Coyote looked more closely at the woman and saw that she was very, very thin and looked half dead.

"I have no food, but why are you starving? If this is the belly of the Giant Monster, then the walls must be his stomach and liver and fat—plenty of food!"

Coyote took out one of his knives and began to carve meat and fat from the walls. He fed it to the woman and to the others who crawled up to the light and the smell of food.

The people began to feel stronger and happier, but not totally happy.

"How can we get out of here, Coyote?" they moaned.

"Don't worry. I'll find the Monster's heart and cut it out. Where is the heart anyway? It must be around here someplace."

The people got very quiet and listened. Far away they could hear a sound—boom-boom, boom-boom, boom-boom...

They followed the sound—boom-boom, boom-boom—down the dark and slippery passages until they came to a huge throbbing mass—BOOM-BOOM, BOOM-BOOM...

Coyote reached into his pack and pulled out all of his sharp knives. He gave four of them to the strongest of the people and kept one for himself.

"Everyone get as close to the mouth as possible. We have to work quickly—when we cut out his heart, the monster will howl and we have to run out of his mouth as fast as we can!"

The five knives began to flash, cutting and stabbing and hacking at the heart. BOOM-BOOM, Boom-boom...blood was flowing out of the heart and pooling around them—up to their ankles, their knees—boom-boom, boom-boom—up to their belly buttons—boom-boom...when suddenly...

"AAAARRRGGHHHHHH!" the Giant Monster screamed.

"RUN!" yelled Coyote, and all of the people ran out the Giant Monster's mouth as his final scream pierced the air. His sharp teeth fell shut—SNAP!—as the last person ran out to safety.

They carved the great monster and Coyote began dealing out portions of the body to various parts of the country all over the land—the heart of the monster toward the south, the liver of the monster toward the north, bits toward the sunrise, pieces toward the sunset.

Old Woman saw what was happening and said, "Coyote, what is the meaning of this? You have distributed all of the body to faraway lands but have left nothing right here!"

Coyote looked around and saw that this was true. Mmmmmm. He turned to the people and said, "Bring me some water to wash my hands." They brought him water and he washed his hands. With the bloody wash water he sprinkled the local regions saying, "The blood of the monster will make you a powerful people."

And so it is that the Nez Perce have been a powerful people forevermore.

And, forevermore, the Heart and Liver of the Monster have remained in the mountains of Idaho, where the rock formations remind the people of Coyote's protection.

"What landforms were mentioned in the story?"
Salmon River, mountains, ridges, rock formations.

"Who can tell us what happened in this story?"
Students paraphrase/summarize the story.

"In this story the Coyote defeats the monster, making the Native Americans more powerful. It also results in the rock formations that were once the Heart and Liver of the Monster. These two rock formations really exist in Idaho, the area where the Nez Perce lived. This story not only told the tribe members about the history of their people, but also helped them recognize and remember landforms that were found along the migratory pattern they traveled each year. The story gives a reason for rocks that are shaped like other objects (in this case the monster's heart and liver)." Show students pictures of the heart and liver rock formations that still stand. (Pictures can be found on the websites listed under resources).

"Do you think this is really how the rock formations were formed? Why or Why not? If not, why do you think the Nez Perce told this story?"

To justify the formations, to explain the powerfulness of the tribe, to teach their history, to help the tribe members learn about the landforms of their area.

"We are going to create a story similar to that of the Nez Perce that incorporates the landforms of our state. The state of Tennessee has many different land and water forms that we have studied. Let's start in West Tennessee and move east." List the land/water forms as the students give them to you. Give students a blank map of Tennessee to draw/label these areas on the map as they go: Mississippi River, Coastal Plain, Highland Rim, Nashville Basin, Cumberland Plateau, Great Valley, Unaka Mountains. Include other areas such as Tennessee River.

"Rock City, near Chattanooga, Tennessee, contains many rock formations. Let's visit the Rock City website listed above and watch the short video on Rock City."

Rock City 1,000-ton Balanced Rock

Rock City Lovers' Leap

Rock City Needle's Eye

"Let's brainstorm some fictional ways that Rock City might have been created, incorporating Coyote as a main character." List the students suggestions on the board. This brainstorming will help the students begin developing their own original tales that incorporate Coyote as a trickster and geographical landforms.

"You're each going write your own story about how Coyote helped to create a landform at Rock City. These are the questions to answer as you brainstorm:

- What two Tennessee landforms will Coyote travel through?
- What animal/creature will he encounter along the way?
- What problem does he have with this creature?
- How does Rock City come about?

"After you have brainstormed answers to these questions, tell your story to a partner, then write a rough draft."

After the rough draft is completed, students will go through the revision process adding figurative language, sound effects, describing words. Next, students will edit and complete their final draft. Students will then practice telling their stories with a partner and as homework. Students will perform their stories for the class. After stories are told, the class will reflect on the landforms that are mentioned in the story and the creation of Rock City.

ASSESSMENT

Basic fictional writing rubrics can be used as the basis of the assessment, with the addition of the accurate use of state landforms and rock formations in the story.

__BRANDI SELF__ has been an educator for thirteen years in Knoxville, TN. Currently she is the district coordinator for the ARTS360 Program which is a federally funded arts integration initiative for Knox County Schools. Previously, Brandi spent 12 years as an intermediate teacher for Knox County Schools. As an educator she always found ways to weave social studies throughout the other curricular areas to promote student interest and achievement. Brandi has presented on the national, state, and district levels in the area of effective teaching practices and student achievement. Brandi and her husband, Bryan, live with their daughter in Knoxville, TN.

The Three Pigs, Revisited:

A GEOGRAPHY LESSON

Jane Stenson

OBJECTIVES *for Grades Two – Five*

Students will

- think critically about a revered folk tale.
- learn and employ the folktale structure.
- change the story's setting and determine how that impacts the story.
- determine that each geographic setting establishes what is (culturally) appropriate for that place.
- tell their newly created story using a storyboard.
- 'play' with plot and setting.

MATERIALS

- typing paper for storyboards
- pencils and colored pencils
- resources for research

INSTRUCTIONAL PLAN

Looking out the window during this rainy and tumultuous spring, I wondered who could live safely in this weather. We had tornadoes and floods and a new storm type, the derecho, which blows sideways from the right at 80+ mph, creates general havoc and power outages. Trees were ripped from the ground and more tornadoes and more rain happened. Simultaneously, I was preparing to tell "The Three Pigs" to a kindergarten class and I really wondered which house was the safest house—the straw, the sticks, or the brick. As it turns out, faced with a wolf that looks like a tornado, no house was safe. We need always to be prepared to live smart in the environment where we're placed, and we need to be good stewards of that environment.

So, what does that mean for a folktale, grounded in layers of environmental and cultural information? Is the secret message of "The Three Pigs" that straw or stick houses are 'less than' and that the people who build them are lazy? Does this mean that the second pig is a non-thinker? He one-upped his brother the first pig by only modestly improving his brother's choice of building material. The third pig is extolled as serious and hard-working, strong enough to withstand adversity; the third pig is the clever pig. Is it coincidence that brick homes tend to be built by people in Western countries and temperate climates, often those with more money? Straw and stick houses are more common in non-European cultures particularly in Africa and Asia.

As a teacher interested in multiculturalism, in having children become world citizens, I have the responsibility to convince children the brick house is important to this story and, simultaneously, not right for every environment/person in the world. Because young children will not understand the brick house as a metaphor, I must introduce other geographic information which demonstrates many ways to establish shelter, a basic human need. Children can understand houses on stilts near the heavy sea, or thatched huts in the tropics or even living in an apartment in a city. In those environments the individual pig's brick house would be inappropriate.

And here's the kicker: "The Three Pigs" is a really good story. The plot is simple and straight-forward. It's easily remembered and the huffing and puffing cries out for audience participation. So, first we'll look at the structure of the story.

ACTIVITY 1 On a six-framed piece of paper, place simple, stick-figured drawings of what occurs, e.g., in frame one *draw* the main character(s) within the setting...and, because of multicultural concerns, remember to show the setting. In frame four draw some solutions to the problem, etc. Take a look at the story in the storyboard format.

ACTIVITY 2 Teacher tells the "The Three Pigs" and children create their storyboard. Mention that almost all folktales use this structure.

ACTIVITY 3 *The Three Little Javelinas* by Susan Lowell is the model I share with the children. It's fun, and it accurately moves the classic European-American tale to the Sonoran Desert, the trickster Coyote's country. The three pigs are javalinas or collared peccaries—a very bristly wild pig. Saguaro cactus bloom and dust storms and thunderheads are prominent. The pigs' houses are brush shelters, sticks and mud, as well as ramadas (roofs with no supporting walls to provide shade) and adobe bricks with a tin roof. Lowell comments that she "tried to handle all of this geographical and cultural material with a light touch." With the children I point out that because we change the setting, there are resultant specific changes in the animals, plants, soil and weather... and housing.

ACTIVITY 4 **The student's turn: Kindergarten – Third Grade:** Provide students with a list of places and at least four sources for each, either books or internet, so they can see pictures of the areas being researched, such as the Amazon rainforest, a Caribbean island, a major metropolitan US city, the veldt, Greenland, Siberia. Have them fill out the grid as much as possible to determine what they know about these regions.

Place	Housing	Climate	Vegetation	Animals	Clothing	Fuel
Amazon rainforest						
Caribbean						
Chicago						
the Veldt						
Greenland						
Siberia						

The student's turn: Grades Four and up: Some of these students may need to use the grid format to broaden their knowledge before trying this activity. Assign students in small groups to keep the three pig plot and change the setting from a temperate, pastoral setting to something different. What ideas can the children entertain? With that decision, ask students to create a new storyboard and add sensory details in each square to construct the environmental changes they envision. First, are there pig-like main characters? Is the wolf-type character available in the new setting, or does wolfie change to a XXX? What three units of housing will appear in the story? What sort of problems can the new antagonist create in this exotic environment? How can the new little 'pigs' defeat the antagonist?

Now, using the storyboard, "tell" your story to the class.

This activity shows students two of the essentials for good writing—setting and plot. We want children to understand the bare bones of good writing. And, we want them to play with the essentials before tackling their own stories. Further, we want their stories filled with accurate and rich sensory details that support the plot and characters. My emphasis on a multicultural approach as a way to appreciate the whole world is a cognitive expression of how to think critically about the stories that govern our lives.

ASSESSMENT

The research grid can be checked for thoroughness and accuracy within the students working groups. The resulting storyboards can be checked for plot structure, sensory details and usability to tell a story. The told story can be enjoyed for the student's imaginative use of geography to create a 'new' story.

RESOURCES

Dorfman, Ariel. *The Empire's Old Clothes or What the Lone Ranger, Babar, and Other Innocent Heroes do to our Minds.* NY: Pantheon, 1983.

Galdone, Paul. *The Three Little Pigs.* NY: Sandpiper. 1984.

Lowell, Susan. *The Three Little Javelinas.* Flagstaff, AZ: Northland Publishing, 1992.

__JANE STENSON__ is coauthor and coeditor of this book! See bio following the articles.

Tall Tales Across the USA

USING STORIES TO UNDERSTAND GEOGRAPHY

Aya Borchers

OBJECTIVES *for Grades One and Two*

Students will

- develop a spatial understanding of geographic characteristics and regions of the United States.
- acquire skills to interpret maps, map symbols, geographic representations and cardinal directions and incorporate technologies to access, process, and report information about the United States.
- recognize how environment affects human systems and how human actions modify physical environment.
- develop an understanding of the characteristics, distribution, migration and settlement of human populations in early America.

MATERIALS

- LARGE map of North America in a central location
- broad range of maps (climate, topographic, political, road, different projections, outdated and current road maps)
- globe(s)
- atlas(es)
- tall tales/trade books
- Google Earth Registration
- iPhone applications, GPS, weather reports, SKYPE, aerial and satellite images, etc.
- models

INSTRUCTIONAL PLAN

Part of an overarching unit on the United States, artfully told tall tales address the Geography National Standards. While tall tales are one of America's major contributions to the oral and literary world, they document the pioneer experience and westward movement of settlers in the early days of our country. A larger than life cast of characters challenges young minds to incorporate cardinal directionality and create a framework of the geographic areas in our country, sites of natural wonders, national landmarks and monuments, and help develop higher level thinking skills to distinguish between fact and farce. Who is Old Muddy? What is the Shortgrass Prairie? Where is Cape Cod? Why are the Smoky Mountains smoky and the waters of the Great Salt Lake salty?

Tall tales capture the quintessential heartiness and industry of the American pioneer. The stories/tales illustrate early settlers' attempts to tame the land and the resulting occupations that contributed to our country's development. Tall tale heroes and heroines feature the courage, compassion, determination, perseverance, sense of humor, independent spirit, thirst for adventure, the need for social justice, space, freedom and survival that made our nation possible.

On Day 1, we tell one tall tale and often begin with "Swamp Angel" (Isaac, 1994). Our discussion at story's end begins with "What are your thoughts, questions and 'noticings'?" At this early stage, responses range from mere delight to astute observations. If responses begin to identify substantive traits, we begin a "what is a tall tale?' chart that will expand throughout the exploration. If not, we present the idea of such a chart and stimulate thinking. (Ask students to consider 'what makes a tall tale a tall tale?' 'What makes a fairy tale a fairy tale?' 'What makes a legend a legend?' We feature our chart in a highly visible and accessible location (computer document projected on an interactive board, dry erase/chalk/bulletin board, chart paper, etc.). We teachers steer discussion, if necessary, to maintain focus and maintain a neutral position with verbal responses such as, 'I like your thinking...' or 'what do you think?' or 'hold that thought, you're onto something....' What we don't do is tell them what a tall tale is. We leave that yet to be determined, so the children can figure it out.

At this point, we may also begin to post and track the exploits of our tall tale characters on our oversized map of the United States. Knowing there are many tales and characters to come, students volunteer to illustrate their interpretation of characters and images that represent their exploits to pin to the map.

While formally introducing the variety of representations available, we model and assist students to recall and locate where characters were born and where their adventures take place.

On Day 2, we read *Mike Fink* (Kellogg, 1992). Students inevitably make connections with the previous tale and share additional questions, comments and notices. We add new ideas to their chart; pin new images to the oversized map; and allow more students to locate regions, states, landmarks, etc. on maps. We use Google Earth and see the Mighty Mississippi! Take time to preview (logistics can be tricky) and with students travel via Google Earth. With our school as the starting point, we pan out and jettison to the Allegheny Mountains, Niagara Falls, the Grand Canyon and other magnificent sites.

On Day 3, we tell the tale of Keelboat Annie. Like Mike Fink, Annie Christmas longs to be and finally becomes a keelboat captain. Unlike, Mike Fink, Keelboat Annie is African American. The commonalities and differences found in these two tales lend themselves to a Venn Diagram.

On Day 4, we introduce *Sally Ann Thunder Ann Whirlwind Crockett* (Kellogg, 1995). Presenting tall tales in this order balances gender and race and familiarizes young readers with the genre from a less than cliché angle. We continue to introduce new tall tales and follow the interests of our students. Inevitably, endless ideas for activities tumble from the children, and we are selective!

Over the course of our study, students demonstrate their understanding in a manner of their choice. Some students may require teacher guidance and support more than others. A summary of characters and geographic elements associated with their tall tale is as follows:

Swamp Angel takes us from the backwoods across the hills of Tennessee and explains the origin of the Great Smoky Mountains. Angel's antics spill over to neighboring Kentucky and move clear across America to Montana's Shortgrass Prairie.

Mike Fink guides us through our nation's mountains, plains and waterways. From the Allegheny Mountains he forges rapids and waterfalls across America, sprints across the Great Plains and trains with grizzlies in the Rocky Mountains

Keelboat Annie, nee Annie Christmas, reinforces the introduction to our nation's waterways as well as defines herself as a strong female African-American tall tale hero. Together with Mike Fink, Keelboat Annie brings the life of a keelboat captain along the Mississippi, Missouri and Ohio waterways down to New Orleans to life.

In addition, Annie Christmas' story speaks for the smaller percentage of free people of color who amassed wealth owning land and ships. Born in our country's South, Annie Christmas heads to New Orleans, overcomes gender and racial discrimination to follow her dream and becomes a keelboat captain.

Sally Ann Thunder Ann Whirlwind Crockett moves from Kentucky to the wild frontier. Her tale describes the region and the culture of living between Minnesota and Louisiana along the Mississippi River. This tale provides perspective with references to Mike Fink and, of course, Davy Crockett.

Paul Bunyan's adventures straddle the country. Beginning with the icy blue winters of the Northeast and the clearing of the once heavily forested Midwest we learn how (and why) the St. Lawrence River connects the Great Lakes to the East Coast and delight in the makings of Niagara Falls, Mammoth Cave in Kentucky, Bryce Canyon in Utah, the Great Sand Dunes in Colorado, Old Faithful in Wyoming, Mt. Rainier in Washington and Big Sur in California. (Some say Paul Bunyan and Babe continue to roam the mountain ranges in Alaska to this day…!)

Pecos Bill heads west from New England and takes us to Texas and the Pecos River. Growing up with coyotes in the wild, Pecos Bill depicts survival amidst trout filled rivers, rocky canyons, caves and the desert.

And, later joining the long standing tall tale tradition of American folklore, Thunder Rose adds to the lesser known part of American history: after the end of the Civil War, Africans-made-slaves in the south who headed west. Thunder Rose's story aptly blossoms in Texas and speaks of the Rio Grande and a cattle drive north up the Chisholm Trail to Abilene.

While New England sea captain Stormalong speaks a good deal of Massachusetts and the Atlantic, his journey includes 'a roughly two thousand mile' walk west and sheds light on the origin of the Great Salt Lake.

Johnny Appleseed, or more correctly, Appleseed John, also hails from New England and charts a trail from Massachusetts across the Allegheny Plateau in Pennsylvania and includes planting and tending trees throughout West Virginia, Ohio and Indiana. Story elements reference overshooting Fort Pitt on a trip down the Allegheny River and the long journey upriver to where the Allegheny meets the Monongahela.

By creating and maintaining the charts, graphs, diagrams and maps that track these tall tale characters who pave their way across the USA, students develop a greater understanding of regions early settlement, map-making, topography, climate, and the relationship between environment and people's lifestyles in early America. Students refine their storytelling skills as they delight in telling and retelling these tall tales complete with geographic references all while demonstrating the five themes of geography: location, place, region, human and environmental interaction, and the movement of goods and services...we arrive at the standards through storytelling!

RESOURCES

Isaacs, Anne. *Swamp Angel.* NY: Dutton Books, 1994.

Erdoes, Richard. *Legends and Tales of the American West.* NY: Pantheon, 1991.

Hurston, Zora Neale. *Lies and Other Tall Tales.* NY: Harpercollins, 2005.

Kellogg, Steven. *Mike Fink: a Tall Tale.* NY: Morrow Junior Books, 1992.

Kellogg, Steven. *Sally Ann Thunder Ann Whirlwind Crockett: a Tall Tale.* NY: Morrow Junior Books, 1995.

Osbourne, Mary Pope. *American Tall Tales.* NY: Alfred A. Knopf, 1991.

San Souci, Robert. *Cut from the Same Cloth: American Women of Myth, Legend and Tall Tale.* NY: Puffin Books, 1993.

AYA BORCHERS *teaches first grade at Baker Demonstration School in Wilmette, IL. Her interest in and commitment to progressive education—child-centered and exploratory—means that this unit on the American Tall Tales has evolved throughout her teaching career under the tutelage of Dr. Terrie Bridgman and on her own. Children continue to tweak, temper and love this exploration of United States geography and story. Aya received her AB from Smith College and her MAT from National-Louis University.*

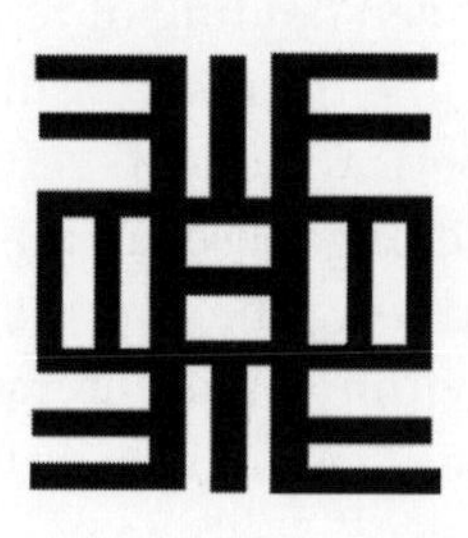

Adinkra nea onnim no sua a ohu
means "Know by Learning"
Proverb: He who does not know can know
by learning. This adinkra represents
knowledge gained through learning.

CHAPTER FOUR

National Council of Social Studies 4. Individual Development & Identity

Social studies programs should include experiences that provide for the study of individual development and identity.

Personal identity is shaped by an individual's culture, by groups, by institutional influences, and by lived experiences shared with people inside and outside the individual's own culture throughout her or his development.

Questions related to identity and development, which are important in psychology, sociology, and anthropology, are central to the understanding of who we are.

The study of individual development and identity will help students to describe factors important to the development of personal identity.

In the early grades, young learners develop their personal identities in the context of families, peers, schools, and communities.

In the middle grades, issues of personal identity are refocused as the individual begins to explain his or her unique qualities in relation to others.

At the high school level, students need to encounter multiple opportunities to examine contemporary patterns of human behavior.

SUSAN O'HALLORAN | MEGAN CAWLEY
JIM WINSHIP & JAMES HARTWICK | BOBBY NORFOLK
SHERRY NORFOLK | ANDY OFFUTT IRWIN
JANE STENSON | DONNA WASHINGTON

Personal and Cultural Identity Through Stories

Susan O'Halloran

All who love children have moments when we wonder if these outrageously self-centered beings will ever enter the civilized world! We watch children refuse to consider that others exist for any reason than to fulfill their needs and, yet, somehow, miraculously, one day they offer to help other children with their homework or ask if we need anything.

While stories can't be given all the credit for this transformation, the narratives that surround children are one of the ways they grow from a 'me-and-only-me' awareness to a collective consciousness. Stories help children make the journey from egocentric newborn to sensitive, contributing member of society.

Successful integration into the larger world starts with growing a sense of self as a discreet, unique and valued entity. Identity-rich stories help children paint a self-portrait, and create images of what they're likely to face, their capacities and dreams. Stories can be the balm for turning bruised egos into generous spirits so that children's self definition includes others. With a foundation of self awareness, children's perceptions expand in rippling concentric circles from the individual to his or her family, to the child's school, neighborhood, place of worship, community groups and, eventually, to the wider society and world.

Simultaneously, an overlay of cultural concentric circles develops, the center being a personal cultural identity and broadening to an awareness, then an understanding of how these various groups form communities, alliances, nations and even universal or "we" identities. Over time, cultural identity becomes part of self-identity. Here I'm using cultural identity to mean a child's sense of place, time, gender, race, history, nationality, sexual orientation, religious beliefs, ethnicity and so on. It is in these cultural circles of identity where storytelling partnered with social studies can give children a most precious gift: a more interrelated, appreciative and generous self... a path toward an humane consciousness.

First, children need to see cultural representations of themselves.

Just as the child starts with a growing sense of "I am," children need a personal cultural self as the basis for forming a positive community identity. Professional storyteller, Anne Shimojima, talks about being raised in the 1950s and what a rare occurrence it was to see Asian Americans on television. Whenever it did happen, someone in her family would shout, "Asian on TV!" Everyone came running to see this astounding sight.

Years later, when she was in her thirties, Anne tells of going to a play that had only two actors. Like her, they were Japanese Americans. In all her childhood and in all her adult life up to that point, Anne had never seen people who were Asian on stage. An odd sensation swept through her body. She says, "Because they were up there on stage, I had this overwhelming feeling that I was there in my seat. It was that profound. Because they were there; I was here." Till that moment, Anne never realized how invisible she had felt. If you grow up and never see anyone who looks like you in the popular culture, Anne says, "It's as if you're looking into the mirror of life and there's no reflection."

Children deserve to know they are real; that they, and people like them, exist. How basic! Yet, teachers and storytellers are overwhelmed by the changing demographics of present-day school children…(there are 43 languages spoken in the homes of students at my local high school.) How to know about all the many cultures present in our classrooms today? Of course, we want to learn as much about the backgrounds of the children as we can. But whether we are responsible for a yearlong class, a weeklong residency or one assembly, we can include the children's voices and experiences as a central part of the curriculum.

At a recent residency, one third grader, after being coached about speaking in images, described her grandfather coming to America each year from Mexico to work. Describing her grandfather picking cotton for 12 hours a day and cutting his fingers and hands on the dried bristles, she said, "He watched the white of the cotton turn red from his blood." Teachers and tellers don't have to know "everything" about the life of migrant workers before they are present in the classroom. Rather, we must let the children tell the class who they are and what their families are like.

Whether children tell stories of how they make tortillas or why they like to go to the mosque on Friday afternoons, simply telling or hearing stories with their cultural markers can avoid the split so many children experience: they feel they are one person at school and another at home. Our students can feel whole or as a hyphenated-American friend of mine said when her culture was finally integrated into her school experience, "I no longer felt as if I was straddling two worlds. Each patch in the quilt of my life was unique but, finally, I felt that I was made of one cloth."

Second, children need to see and experience other cultures.

As children hear stories from classmates, they start to understand that others in their schools and community are both individuals and part of groups as well. Having felt culturally seen and valued, now children can see and value each other and the groups to which their friends belong.

As teachers, professional storytellers and children share their own cultural backgrounds we are able to break down the notion that any one group is more "strange" than another or even more "exotic." Through stories, people who are culturally different become familiar friends ("Why they're just like me!") and, simultaneously, people with unique experiences. Holding this both/and of cultures—we are alike and we are different from each other - generates a truer appreciation than the unrealistic and often unintentionally disrespectful attempts at color blindness.

This mutual sharing is important because we want to remember that the dominant culture (whatever that may be in any given time or place) can be equally strange and confusing to students who aren't identified as part of the majority. Professional storyteller Arif Choudhury who is Bangladeshi American and Muslim, tells of attending an elementary school where the students were predominantly Jewish. He saw his classmates playing with dreidels and assumed "it was just some kind of game that white people played." However, Arif's friend, Christopher, who was white and Christian, said he didn't know what a dreidel was either. Arif was stunned to discover that there was more than one kind of "white people."

As teachers and storytellers we mean well by introducing a culture to our students but, because our knowledge can be superficial or our time is short, we may fall into the trap of introducing a new culture with just one or two identifiable attributes and, therefore, unintentionally create new stereotypes. Storytelling done well shows that there is massive diversity within every culture. Olga Loya's parents did not approve of her identifying with her Indian heritage. Nancy Wang's mother didn't agree with her style of dress or choice of profession. Arif Choudhury's cousins didn't believe he was following Islamic rituals correctly and accused him of "not being Muslim enough." These stories let children know that there are many ways to be Mexican, Chinese, Muslim and any other kind of American.

Third, children need to see their group throughout history.

Moving outward to the further rings of cultural identity, students need to see their groups involved in the national and world arenas. Telling the stories of *every group* within the social studies curricula can move children from being passive spectators to actors on the stage of life when they see that their group has been and is active. For example, Anne not only missed knowing that Asian people existed as present day members of society; she missed the stories of her group as active participants in the great march of history.

Just as children must develop a sense of pride about who they are individually, they need a cultural identity that says they come from people who have accomplished great things, resisted oppression and clung to their humanity no matter what de-humanizing traumas they faced. Being awarded this recognition, they are able to extend similar attributes and appreciation to other groups.

These stories make historical events truer and more exciting while demonstrating that it is ordinary people who make history. Yes, we need children to hear the stories of Dr. King, Rosa Parks, Caesar Chavez and so on, but students need to know that many people not in the history books faced great fears and, yet, developed their bravery over time. Plus, the greats and the less known came from and were supported by communities of people who have always worked to make the world a better place. Through the stories of everyday people working for change, children learn that making a difference is possible for them as well.

Fourth, children learn they are part of a larger group called humanity.

With experience and stories children can develop a communal and universal identity that supersedes and enhances their group identity. Stories can move children to the outer circle of cultural identity, the "we." Students learn that they are part of their specific group and time but, like many before them, they can also answer the call to a higher moral order and connectivity with all human beings.

Let me give you two examples:

In 1857, the citizens of Oberlin, Ohio lived in a time when many supported slavery, yet seven hundred of them defied the U.S. Government's Fugitive Slave Law—risking fines and imprisonment—by refusing to allow John Price to be re-captured into bondage.

More recently, many US citizens were swayed by the anti-Muslim fervor that swept the country after the September 11th terrorist attacks. However, other citizens took a stand in defense of their Muslim neighbors declaring that we are one diverse nation and our collective strength comes from that diversity.

Social studies is all about storytelling. Who gets to tell the story? What is the point of view? And, what or who is the story about? America is a bold experiment in democracy founded on a diverse population. People from all over the world choose to come here. Developing a personal and an American identity is not for the faint of heart. But it is the storytelling in social studies that empowers students, showing them that they are part of something larger than their individual selves. Developing a cultural as well as a personal identity allows children to feel connected to those who came before them, to those surrounding them now, and to a future we can build together.

NOTE: Excerpts from the professional tellers' stories mentioned in this article can be found at: www.racebridgesvideos.com.

***SUSAN O'HALLORAN** is a writer, story artist, seminar leader and keynote speaker whose work explores the complex issues of social justice through entertainment and story. She is author of four books and producer of curricula, performances and films including Black, White and Brown: Tribes & Bridges at the Steppenwolf Theatre and More Alike Than Not: Stories of Three Americans—Catholic, Jewish and Muslim. The Chicago Reader says O'Halloran "has mastered the Irish art of telling stories that are funny and heart-wrenching at the same time." Susan has been a National Storytelling Network keynote speaker, a featured teller at the National Storytelling Festival in Jonesborough, TN and a recipient of the NSN Circle of Excellence Oracle Award. She lives in Evanston, Illinois and can be found at: www. susanohalloran.com.*

Storytelling and Personal Histories

Megan R. Cawley

The essence of social studies is the relationship of the stories of people's lives, livelihoods and environments with the big social and political events. It is the stories and the storytelling surrounding the big events that allow students to deconstruct what is happening to both the heroes and the common man. Knowledge of a multitude of points of view and a compassionate approach to each other is vital for our future leaders.

As teachers, we remember back to our own middle school history classes and our history text book which were full of dry facts and dates. Lots of dates. Text books were the only route to understanding and transmitting information about culture and events. Text books did not allow the student to question or to see how past culture connected to their own culture. When asked "why do we study history?" a common response from adults and students alike is "to avoid making the same mistakes." But, unless the student has experiential knowledge of the past there isn't a lasting and real understanding, and the student can't make sense of what happened in the past in order to avoid it happening in the future. This is where the infinite value of storytelling comes in.

Experiencing lives in other contexts provides a lasting way to view history and it provides an opening of the student's mind to new possibilities. Much like traveling into a new country, stories and storytelling present the opportunity to experience as yet unknown territories and people. Simultaneously, in middle school, students question their personal identity, or who they are. Their identity has been shaped by family, culture and environment—by experiences out of school but especially in school. It is important to provide experiences that help the students formulate their personal identity while recognizing others' identities as separate from themselves. The idea of helping each student view himself and every person as unique and deserving is a good start toward compassionate citizenship.

A common and easy way to help students connect with course content is the use of a story from the time period within the course of study, such as the epic Gilgamesh while studying Mesopotamia. It is after all the story of the first superhero! Students readily connect to the idea of having superpowers. Another way is to read historical fiction. *The Secrets of Vesuvius* is a wonderful story by Sara Louise Clark Bisel with additional contributions by Shelley Tanaka and Jane Bisel that tells of the excavation and analysis of the skeleton and other artifacts found in the archeology site at Herculaneum, a town near Pompeii. Based on archeologist's actual findings, this fictional story about a teenage slave also evolved from their work. Beyond learning the *content* of a culture, historical fiction encourages students to use their imaginations to make connections to history. From a new series *You Wouldn't Want to be a...* (many titles, written by many authors) I used...*be a slave in Ancient Greece* to infuse humor to help students understand a different time period.

INSTRUCTIONAL PLAN

The most potent way I have found for my eighth graders to analyze the culture of a different time is to understand the causes and consequences of the actions that took place in the personal stories of both the survivors and victims of the Holocaust. The real life stories of real people, especially if they are from the student's age group, creates a strong sense of identification and allows the student to create understanding from an unfathomable situation. We learn from these personal histories in three ways.

First, every year, as part of our study of the Holocaust we travel to the Illinois Holocaust Museum. Our students have been going there since before it was built. How can this be? Before the fabulous new museum was built in its current location on 9603 Woods Drive, Skokie, Illinois, there was a small museum made up of three or four storefronts located on Main Street in Skokie. In the 1970s, the Nationalist Socialist Party of America, a neo-Nazi group, applied for a permit to march. This horrified the residents of Skokie which has a large Holocaust survivor population. They decided they had been silent long enough and that they needed to get their stories heard. They generously donated cultural artifacts - family pictures and possessions in order to "tell" their stories. Further, they donated their storytelling - time to speak to visitor groups. Their storytelling continues at the new museum, and survivors provide outreach to local community groups and schools. Because it has been over 65 years since the end of World War II, the current survivor speakers were all children at the time. They talk about the practicalities of their situations. They talk about the heart-wrenching decisions and sacrifice their families or others, even strangers, made to protect them. They talk about the horrors they faced and the choices they made in order to survive. These stories are vital for my students to hear. It's so personal, as if my students' grandparents were telling them the stories of what happened when they were young.

In addition to survivor accounts my students will hear from professional storytellers. Syd Lieberman tells of his personal reaction to the Nazis' planned march in Skokie in his story "When the Nazis Came" (to Skokie). It is a connection for the students to hear how a calm and respected adult was overcome by feelings of outrage. Storyteller Anne Shimojima tells "Hana's Suitcase" to show students the compassion of Japanese children toward a Holocaust victim. See Shimojima's article on page 20.

The third way stories are incorporated is by using the Personal Identification Cards found on the U.S. Holocaust Museum website. The U.S. Holocaust Museum created information sources for teachers to access the stories of young people who experienced the Holocaust. While there are many lessons designed for teachers on the Museum's websites, I found the following a very effective use of stories and storytelling for my eighth grade students and is an example of how the Museum's resources can be used. Because of their emotional power, I use this as my last lesson and it is part of my assessment for the unit.

OBJECTIVES *for Grade Eight*

Students will

- understand the importance of one person, and the value of personal identity and personal responsibility.
- use their previous knowledge on the socially transmitted beliefs, values of the dominant culture and its disallowance of diverse cultures in its attempts to secure its own race as superior, as promulgated by personal stories in order to draw implications for the present.
- create narratives from non-fiction information through shared materials.

MATERIALS

- print out Identity Cards from the Education section for teachers at http://www.ushmm.org/education/foreducators/story/.
- review the 37 cards and choose 20-25 that will cover a broad range of experiences.
- paste each onto cardboard to make it durable and authentic.
- pencil and paper.

STEPS

1. Randomly let the student choose his/her card.
2. Give a few minutes for the students to read and think about their person. Then I tell them they will share their story in which they will answer these questions:
   a. Summarize in writing what happened to "you" without rewriting the card, and
   b. What do you feel?
   c. Do you think something else could have happened and changed the outcome?
   d. Connect this story to something we have learned about recently (our current events during this unit concentrates on events pertaining to possible genocides).
3. We then share. The students are each, in effect, telling a story about an actual person. Interestingly, there will be a few who will try to rewrite history to save their person but others in the group will argue why or why not that rewrite would be possible. Several will be able to connect it to current day situations or recent past genocides.
4. At the end of class collect the writings. Ask the class why we did this lesson and what was its value?

Stories in their many forms, whether literature from a certain culture, stories read to the students and written by others, stories written and read by students, storytellers or survivors, are vital to the Middle School students' understanding and learning about other cultures and the changes, and continuity across time. The creation of empathy is the core of this understanding and the retention of this knowledge by the student so it can be utilized in their lives.

RESOURCES

Armento, Beverly J., et al. *A More Perfect Union.* Boston, MA: Houghton Mifflin Company, 1999.

Bisel, Sara Louise Clark. *The Secrets of Vesuvius.* NY: Scholastic Inc., 1990.

"Epic of Gilgamesh"—any edition, Hakim, Joy. *A History of US.* NY: Oxford University Press, Inc., 2003

Illinois Holocaust Museum. http://www.ushmm.org/education/foreducators/story.

Levine, Karen. *Hana's Suitcase: A True Story.* Toronto, Canada: Second Story Press, 2002.

"When the Nazis Came." Lieberman, Syd. *Streets and Alleys.* CD. Found at www.sydlieberman.com

McDonald, Fiona. *You Wouldn't Want to Be a Slave in Ancient Greece!* NY: Franklin Watts, 2001. This series of books were created and designed by David Salariya and illustrated by David Antram.

Currently teaching Middle School Social Studies at the Baker Demonstration School in Wilmette, IL, ***MEGAN CAWLEY*** *previously taught in the Winnetka Public Schools. Her prior background(s) as lawyer and mother enables her to establish clear expectations for academic and social/emotional growth of her students. Her teaching is full of challenging and creative activities that allows all students to be successful, and she maintains a dialogue with families to foster the shared responsibility between home and school. A BA from Northwestern University, JD from DePaul University School of Law and an MAT from National-Louis University means her teaching goal is to impart a love of learning and the ability to ask questions and seek answers about the world.*

Using Story to Understand the Reality of Undocumented Latino Youth

Jim Winship and James Hartwick

OBJECTIVES *for Grades Six – Eight (middle school) social studies*

Students will

- identify and critically analyze arguments in favor and opposed to providing in-state tuition for undocumented immigrants.
- explain the differences between rights that all people living in the United States have and privileges reserved for citizens of the United States.
- listen to and learn from their peers in their groups.
- discuss this controversial issue in a respectful and appropriate manner.
- identify areas of agreement and disagreement with other students and generate consensus in groups on some aspect of this issue upon which they can agree.
- explain and provide support for their individual position in a clear, one to two page essay,
- empathize with Christian and the expensive educational opportunities faced by him and other undocumented immigrants.
- identify options for informing and persuading others and government officials of their views.

MATERIALS

- Christian's story
- Structured Academic Controversy (SAC) methodology

Christian's Story

Written by one of the authors after interviewing Christian who just graduated from high school. This story can be used for instructional purposes.

Christian was in middle school in a Wisconsin city six years ago, and asked his father one day why they did not go back to Mexico to visit relatives. Other students in his school, also Mexican-Americans, would go back across the border to visit relatives. That was when his father first told him that they were not citizens. They were undocumented immigrants—persons who did not have the legal visas or permission to live in the United States.

When Christian was five, he had come to New York City to live with his father. "Where we lived in New York, there were so many people who spoke Spanish. Speaking Spanish at home, in the community [was the norm]. It was not until I started school, at P.S. 106, that I started to learn and speak English."

"When I was in third grade, 9/11 happened—it did not seem that far from the school." A while after that, we came to Wisconsin."

When one looks at Christian's life, at first glance it seems the same immigrant success story that has played over and over in America for centuries—the child who starts school not knowing English, learns the language, graduates from high school, looks forward to going to college, and being a productive adult. Christian has been a good student, has mentored a middle school student, is active politically, and has been planning to attend a Wisconsin state university, majoring in English.

Casting a shadow over this story is that Christian is undocumented, and in 2011 getting a college education in Wisconsin is even more problematic for undocumented students than it has been. In 2009, the Wisconsin legislature passed a law allowing undocumented students graduating from Wisconsin high schools to pay in-state rather than out-of-state tuition, a difference of about $7500 in tuition. As undocumented students are not eligible for most state and federal aid, the in-state tuition was an incentive to continue their education.

continued

When Scott Walker was elected as Wisconsin's governor in 2010 and Republicans gained a majority in both houses of the legislature, one of the provisions they enacted was to repeal this law. This affects about 100 undocumented students currently attending the thirteen state universities in Wisconsin. Christian says with this legislation passed, "Maybe I will attend a technical school—it is less expensive."

Christian also says that in a way "being undocumented is a blessing. My philosophy is 'Don't give up. Try harder than anyone else.'"

One way in which Christian works hard is to advocate for himself and for other undocumented students. He worked hard to get the Dream Act (acronym for Development, Relief and Education for Alien Minors) passed, and lamented when this legislation passed the United States House but was not passed by the Senate in 2010. Christian has spoken out at rallies in Wisconsin on immigration issues, not only at those events sponsored by the immigration rights group Voces de la Frontera but also at a large rally in Madison protesting Governor Walker's actions.

Christian says that his father says that "Every day here is a blessing," and Christian wants those days in the United States to not end. "This is my country, which I call home; I have lived here all my life. However, every day when I wake up, I feel at home, and during the day, things happen that make me feel like an outsider." He won't give up, and states his philosophy is "the fight is worth more than the actual victory."

Christian is one of 11.2 million undocumented persons here in the United States. Many youth are in Christian's situation. Their parents came here in the 1990s, during a period of great economic growth. At that time, it was not difficult to get into the United States, and until 9/11, there were very few efforts to send undocumented persons back to their countries of origin if they had not broken criminal laws (robbery, assault, etc.).

INSTRUCTIONAL PLAN

This lesson plan utilizes the Structured Academic Controversy (SAC) methodology, a cooperative learning and discussion strategy developed by Johnson and Johnson. This strategy focuses on a controversial public issue, i.e., an issue that is of public concern upon which intelligent people can reasonably disagree. In this case, the issue is "Should our democracy extend government support for higher education to undocumented immigrants who—as young people—entered the country illegally?" The SAC approach is designed to help students critically examine both sides of an issue and come to consensus on some aspect of the controversial issue.

A SAC lesson typically begins with a "hook activity" of some type to pique students' interests and to provide important background knowledge about the issue, i.e., Christian's story.

- The focus question, in a binary (i.e., pro/con) form is posted or listed publicly in the classroom. Students are assigned to groups of four, and then to partnerships within each group. One partnership in each group is assigned to carefully read an article and prepare arguments for the pro side of the issue, and the other partnership in each group is assigned to do likewise with the con side of the issue. The teacher provides students with short readings to help them generate a list of the strongest arguments in support of the position to which they have been assigned.
- When the partnerships are ready, each pro partnership presents the pro arguments to the other "audience" partnership in their group of four.
- When the presentation is completed, the audience partnership can ask questions for clarification so that they can better understand the arguments; however, to be clear, this is not meant to be a debate.
- Next, each con group presents the con arguments.
- After this, using notes taken from the presentation of the opposite partnership and perhaps reviewing the opposite pair's readings, each pair presents the arguments of the opposite partnership back to that pair (i.e., the original pro group presents the con arguments and vice versa).

- Once each partnership is knowledgeable about the arguments in support of each side of the issue, the groups are released from their assigned roles, and each group of four in now charged with discussing the issue and trying to come to consensus on at least some aspect of the issue. To be clear, the groups do not have to artificially come to agreement on their overall position on the issue, but rather they are assigned to come to consensus on some aspect of the issue (e.g., which arguments are strongest, or which evidence they would need to reach a more informed opinion). In addition, each group should identify the primary areas of disagreement.
- Now that the students are well informed and had a chance to discuss the issue and to generate partial consensus, the teacher facilitates a class discussion of the issue. To open this class discussion, each group shares what their groups' consensus items were and the sources of their disagreements. Following the class discussion, the teacher conducts a debrief with the class on how well they worked, learned, and discussed together. For assessment, students are typically assigned to in some way communicate a well-supported position on the issue.

In this "college tuition rates for undocumented students" lesson, we have added an enrichment activity to the basic SAC procedure in order to help students empathize with the plight of Christian. After completing the formal SAC lesson, we suggest that you assign students to re-read Christian's story and discuss the questions found in the Assessment section.

When introducing this enrichment activity, the teacher should clarify that it is possible to empathize with the plight of an individual and maintain a position on a policy issue that may negatively impact that individual. Citizens are often faced with difficult choices in which positive and negative consequences must be carefully weighed. In any case, empathy and clear thinking about policy issues are both compatible and desirable outcomes. For example, a student could indicate that he does not support in-state tuition for undocumented students, but nevertheless has ideas as to how Christian might be supported to realize his potential. Or another student might wish to advocate politically enabling undocumented students to pay only in-state tuition to attend college. It is an important civic lesson to learn that there are many ways to advocate for one's position and to support others. Returning to the personal story of Christian allows students to empathize, to value the contributions of others, and to find ways politically or otherwise to support residents of our country. This teaches students to value others, to be aware of the implicit interconnection between people, and to seek the common good.

Tuition protest rally in Madison, WI

Why introduce a personal story, a story of a real person living now, into a social studies lesson plan? One reason, according to the researcher Roger Schank in *Tell Me a Story*, the brain processes stories differently than it processes facts. When we hear a story, we make associations with parts of the story. In reading Christian's story, we may think of times when we were graduating from high school, of things that our fathers told us, about where we were on September 11, 2001. All these associations are stored in parts of our brains, and that helps us to remember the story later on. Many students who do this exercise and look up material to support their positions a month later will not be able to remember all the specific data that supports their positions. Almost all will remember the description of Christian, as it is a story.

A second reason for using this story is that it personalizes the issue. Depending on the school, there may be undocumented students in the class, or it may be a school with some undocumented students, or none of the students may know anyone who is undocumented. In the latter case, after reading the story, students are more likely to be able to think of the issue as one that affects individual people, not just a nameless and faceless group of people.

ASSESSMENT

Assessment can occur in two separate ways. For individual assessment, the teacher can construct and then grade worksheets with the following questions. One worksheet, perhaps front and back, would have the students answering these questions:

(Going beyond opinion and using resources to support your position)

- Should our democracy extend government support for higher education to undocumented immigrants who—as young people—entered the country illegally?
- What steps could you take to inform and potentially persuade others and government officials of your views?

Engage the students' empathic understanding of the situation by having them answer the following questions:

- How would you feel if you were in Christian's position? Explain.
- From what you have read, do you think Christian can make a valuable contribution to our country?
- In light of the fact that the current law in Wisconsin requires Christian and other undocumented immigrants to pay out-of-state tuition, what can be done (individually, with service groups, politically, etc.) for Christian?

There can also be a group assessment of the process, as to how successful the students were in listening to and learning from their peers in their groups, in discussing this controversial issue in a respectful and appropriate manner, and in identifying areas of agreement and disagreement within the group.

REFERENCES & RELATED RESOURCES

Johnson, D.W., & Johnson, R.. *Creative controversy: Intellectual conflict in the classroom* (3rd ed.) Edina, MN: Interaction, 1995.

Schanck, Roger. *Tell Me a Story: Narrative and Intelligence,* Evanston, IL: Northwestern University Press, 2000.

http://www.deliberating.org <http://www.deliberating.org/>. Go to Lessons, then Lessons Procedures on this website. *A more detailed exposition of this procedure is described (including a video showing the Structured Academic Controversy in a classroom).*

http://www.deliberating.org/index.php/resources-topmenu-53/58-educating-non-citizens. *Excellent resources for understanding both sides of this issue.*

"Support for the Dream Act" or "Opposition to the Dream Act." One example of strong opposition is: http://www.humanevents.com/article.php?id=39091. *For more information from the perspectives of those supporting and opposing higher education for undocumented students,*

http://pewhispanic.org/reports. *For information on Latinos/Hispanics in the United States.*

JIM WINSHIP, PH.D. *is professor of social work at the University of Wisconsin-Whitewater. He has worked with Latino parents through parent involvement activities in Southeastern Wisconsin for several decades. He is also a professional storyteller, with an emphasis on bilingual English/Spanish stories*

JAMES M.M. HARTWICK, PH.D. *is an associate professor and the Secondary Social Studies Program coordinator at the University of Wisconsin-Whitewater. He serves on the executive board of the Religion and Education SIG for the American Educational Research Association (AERA) and as a vice president for the Wisconsin Council for the Social Studies. His scholarly work addresses democratic deliberation and discussion, inquiry, reflection, the spiritual and religious lives of teachers, and cultivating a critical and transformative multicultural perspective.*

Shadowball

THE STORY OF THE NEGRO NATIONAL LEAGUES

Bobby Norfolk

"Ain't no man can avoid being born average, but there ain't no man got to be common."
SATCHEL PAIGE

Satchel Paige wasn't common. He was a baseball legend in his own time—a time of Jim Crow laws and enforced racial segregation. His story has a surreal quality that is still riveting today, and which glaringly exposes the injustices of those troubled times.

The inspiration to research, write, and perform a one-man show on Satchel Paige and Negro League Baseball came when I was listening to author Larry Tye being interviewed on the National Public Radio program Fresh Air about his new book *Satchel: The Life and Times of an American Legend* (Random House, 2009). Even though I did not call myself an avid baseball fan, and never followed the season, I do have an intrinsic love for history—and, like most kids, I loved playing softball in my youth, so the interest was there. When I heard Larry Tye discuss how his book about Satchel Paige interwove the sport of baseball with the history of America, I recognized an excellent opportunity to teach American history (1850-1948) through the prism of "The National Pastime."

Satchel Page

As a performer of historical narratives, my first responsibility is to learn as much as I can about the person I will portray and the times in which he lived. Each historical program I develop requires months of research—not only do I want to develop an accurate and engaging performance, but I need to be able to answer any questions that the performance evokes in my listeners (and in my own mind!). So, research began.

I borrowed the Ken Burns *Baseball* (PBS 2010) DVD series from the library—a cinematic masterpiece through which Burns uses baseball to depict the whole of American society in microcosm. I saw how our heritage is uniquely tied to baseball through civil rights, war, peace, national and international politics, and social justice.

I took a year to research the topic of baseball through books, CDs, cassettes, DVDs, and primary sources. Connie Brooks, daughter of James "Cool Papa" Bell, lives in New York, and I called her twice for research. On each occasion, I was taken on a three-hour excursion into baseball history! I was so engaged in her stories that every so often she would ask me, "Are you still there, Mr. Norfolk?" It was a rare treat to listen to this lady speak for six hours with passion and love for her great Dad (on and off the field)—simply priceless!

I kept meticulous notes on the history of the game which I developed into a chronological flow of how America evolved from the Jim Crow era to the point of "re-integrating" the game with Jackie Robinson. (American baseball was integrated from its early beginnings in the late 1880s with African-American players Moses Fleetwood Walker, Frank Grant, and Bud Fowler. They were harassed, threatened, and put upon with violent, unsportsman-like conduct by white players and fans until forced to leave the game altogether. Soon after that, a secret meeting was held by the white owners of the major leagues—their mission: to remove any Negro players from their teams and not hire anymore. This so-called "Gentlemen's Agreement" lasted for almost 60 years preceding Jackie Robinson's ascent to the majors.) These notes would become the foundation of my Story Theatre performance.

During my research, it became clear to me that I would have two narrators rather than just one: James "Cool Papa" Bell and Leroy "Satchel" Paige. Satchel and Cool Papa had an extraordinary experience in race and culture while traveling throughout the U.S. and Latin America from 1922-1949. During those years, Paige and Bell played throughout the regular season in the U.S. and continued through the "winter leagues" in Latin America. In strong contrast to the conditions imposed by American Jim

Crow laws, in Latin America, the Black players ate in five-star restaurants, stayed in luxury hotels with no restrictions, swam on the beaches, and visited any public facilities they wanted to. This gave them a taste of equality, and an understanding of how economics was paramount over the color of one's skin. Back at home, they were once again forced to eat cold cuts and crackers on the road. They sometimes played three or four games per day, then climbed back on the bus without the benefit of shower or bath, only to travel on dusty back roads to another town to play the next day. If they could not find a Colored motel to sleep in, they slept on the cramped bus. Their love and commitment for the game made them persevere!

"They said I was the greatest pitcher
they ever saw...I couldn't understand why
they couldn't give me no justice."
SATCHEL PAIGE

The injustices of the times were certainly startling and heartbreaking. Such violent contrast in treatment of the players based simply on the color of their skin is outrageous to think about in this day and time, but was completely accepted by almost everyone in the 30s and 40s. I felt that it was important to help students understand what social injustice can look like—for them to experience it vicariously through the story of two talented and courageous men, and to empathize with their plight—so that they would recognize and be unwilling to accept it if they encounter it in their own world.

As I learned more and more about Satchel and Cool Papa, their personalities came through clearly to me. My job was to bring these colorful players to life for the audience, allowing their distinct voices to be heard. Watching, listening to, and reading interviews with Satchel helped me develop my depiction of him. As author Larry Tye said, Satchel was "a philosopher, preacher, comedian, and a master storyteller." It was very easy to "hear and see" this man's personality through the book and the audio recording of the book—and, he has been so widely quoted that it was easy to use his own words throughout my script.

The long conversations with Connie Brooks provided the basis for my portrayal of Cool Papa—she imitated his voice and inflections and described his mannerisms so well that he became vivid in my mind.

Beverly Brennan, who teaches Theatre at Harris/Stowe State University, was my director (and her dad was the legendary sportscaster for the St. Louis Cardinals: the late Jack Buck). Her insights and guidance helped immensely in shaping and polishing the story and defining the characters.

The amazing careers of these two outstanding players provide the backdrop for American students to witness the rampant segregation of this era in the US and contrast it with the "parallel universe" that the African-American players experienced in Latin America—the same "parallel universe" in which the white major league players lived back in the States. This profound juxtaposition brings the injustices of the Jim Crow laws into sharp focus, helping students understand more deeply the need for tolerance, equality, and social justice.

Bobby Norfolk in Shadowball

RESOURCES

Burns, Ken. "Baseball: A Film by Ken Burns" (Includes the Tenth Inning). DVD. PBS, 2010.

Gay, Timothy. *Satch, Dizzy, and Rapid Robert.* NY: Simon & Schuster, 2010.

Holway, John. *The Complete Book of Baseball's Negro Leagues: The Other Half of Baseball History.* Fern Park, FL: Hastings House, 2001.

Holway, John B. *Josh and Satch: The Life and Times of Josh Gibson and Satchel Paige.* Westport, CT: Meckler, 1991.

Lester, Larry. *Black Baseball's National Showcase: The East-West All Star Game—1933-1953.* Lincoln, NE: University of Nebraska, 2001.

McCormack, Shaun. *James Cool Papa Bell: A Biography.* NY: Rosen Central, 2002.

Nelson, Kadir. *We Are the Ship: The Story of Negro League Baseball.* NY: Hyperion Books for Children, 2008.

O'Neil, Buck. *I Was Right on Time.* NY: Simon & Schuster, 1996.

Paige, Leroy, John G. Howay and David Lipman. *Maybe I'll Pitch Forever.* Lincoln, NE: Bison Books, 1993.

Peterson, Robert. *Only the Ball was White: A History of Legendary Black Players and All Black Professionals.* NY: Oxford University Press, 1992.

Tye, Larry. *Satchel: The Life and Times of an American Legend.* NY: Random House, 2009.

Ward, Geoffrey and Ken Burns. *Baseball: an Illustrated History.* NY: Alfred A. Knopf, 1994.

PRIMARY RESOURCES

Connie Brooks, daughter of James Cool Papa Bell. Telephone interviews, November 2009 and June 2010.

Bennie Lewis, former intern at the Baseball Hall of Fame in Cooperstown, NY, and the Negro Baseball Hall of Fame in Kansas City, MO. Live interviews, October 2009- August 2010.

Larry Lester, Baseball historian from Kansas City, MO. Live interviews, November 2009 and February 2010.

BOBBY NORFOLK, *an internationally known story performer and teaching artist, is a three-time Emmy Award winner and Parents' Choice honoree. He is one of the most popular and dynamic story-educators in America today! Find out more at www.bobbynorfolk.com.*

Barnstormers

VOICES FROM THE NEGRO BASEBALL LEAGUES AND THE MAJOR LEAGUES

Sherry Norfolk

OBJECTIVES *for Middle School and High School*

Students will

- research, develop, and orally present a fictional dialogue between a Negro League and a Major League baseball player which accurately reflects the conditions of the era.

MATERIALS

- biographies of baseball players from the Negro Leagues and from the Major leagues, circa 1924-1960.
- historical material on the Negro Leagues and Major Leagues.
- internet access highly recommended.

INSTRUCTIONAL PLAN

Bobby's portrayal of "Cool Papa" Bell and Satchel Paige allows students to listen to and learn from the voices of humanity. Listeners are drawn into the story of the triumphs and tribulations of these amazing players, empathizing fully with their experiences.

Curiosity has been provoked—learning follows!

Bobby's narrative provides a glimpse into the story of Negro League baseball; delving further into this fascinating era in American sports reveals a rich and colorful story which had profound impact not only on our national pastime, but upon America's social and moral development. I want students to explore the issues of civil justice, tolerance, and equality that Bobby's performance has raised. Barnstorming provides the perfect platform.

"Back in the day," barnstorming was put together by white Major League players such as J. Hanna "Dizzy" Dean and Bob Feller. They would rent major league stadiums across America, and invite the negro players to that town to play in "All Star" games. The promoters got their pay off the top, and after expenses everyone made a nice salary. Black teams never faced white teams during the baseball season, but they often did so during those barnstorming tours, allowing players to measure and appreciate each others' skills and abilities; however, the white and black players went their separate ways after each game.

With Bobby's help, I developed a list of 15-20 baseball players from the Negro Leagues and the white Major Leagues who had played each other during those barnstorming tours (see list below). Research material was then collected from online and book resources. I raided public library and school library shelves to gather as much print material as possible, and printed out pages from various websites.

White Major League Players

Babe Ruth
Ty Cobb
Honus Wagner
Joe DiMaggio
Lou Gehrig
Ted Stevens
Jerome Hanna "Dizzy" Dean
Paul Dean
A.B. "Happy" Chandler
Charles Cominsky
Branch Rickey
Cy Young
Leo Durocher
Bob Feller
Connie Mack
Stan Musial
Enus "Country" Slaughter
"Peewee" Reese
Whitey Herzog

Negro League Players

Norman "Turkey" Stearns
Ted "Double-Duty" Radcliffe
John "Mule" Suttles
Moses Fleetwood Walker
Ray Dandridge
John Henry "Pop" Lloyd
William Julius "Judy" Johnson
Jake Stevens
Chet Brewer
Oscar Charleston
Satchel Paige
James "Cool Papa" Bell
Larry Doby
Josh Gibson
Bud Fowler
Buck Leonard
Buck O'Neil

To begin this project, I ask the students to share briefly some of their most vivid memories of Bobby's performance. Their list is always long, and always includes the students' outrage at the way the Negro League players were treated.

We then talk about barnstorming (mentioned in the performance). We discuss not only what it was, but the opportunity it provided for some of the best players in the country of any color to face each other on the playing field.

It has to be pointed out that, with the segregated lines drawn so tightly, the players didn't often meet or talk off the field; however, it's fascinating to conjecture what those encounters would've been like if they had taken place. Let's go back in (hypothetical) time...

At this point, a model is required—a demonstration of the type of product I expect and hope for students to produce. As a teaching artist, I ask the classroom teacher to join me in performing an imaginary dialogue between Satchel Paige and Dizzy Dean:

SATCHEL: How-do, Mr. Dean. Ready to lose another ballgame?

DIZZY: Get out there and do what you can, Satch—and I'll do what I can do. We'll see who does it better.

SATCHEL: Well, I don't know what you're going to do, Mr. Dean, but I'm not going to give up any runs if we have to stay here all night.

DIZZY: Where are you-all staying the night, anyhow?

SATCHEL: Well, some of us are sleeping up in the hayloft yonder, but I got a real nice place in the rooming house down the street. I reckon you-all are in the ho-tel?

DIZZY: First class all the way for us! We got clean linens on the bed, 24-hour room service, and hot and cold running water! The boys are eating caviar and drinking fine whiskey.

SATCHEL: We got hot and cold running cockroaches, is what we got. Say, how did your boys get here today? We had us a time getting here in our old bus. Dust flying in the windows like to smother us. Course, if we win tonight the boarding house said all of us can clean up there after the game. We won't likely have much HOT water, but we won't be covered in dust and sweat and grime, neither. And stretching out in the hayloft beats trying to sleep on the bus.

DIZZY: Well, I guess I shouldn't tell you 'bout our ride here on the train—we had us a time in the dining car—they let us stay in there eating steaks and drinking champagne all afternoon, then we moved on to our sleeper cars and got some rest so we could wipe you out this afternoon.

SATCHEL: I reckon they know we don't need no rest to wipe you out this afternoon. Good thing, 'cause we didn't get no rest, bouncing around in that old bus with all the dust and fumes, eating bag lunches our wives and sweethearts packed for us. We'll be lucky to get boloney and crackers and sardines this evening, 'cause we're running low on the home-cooked.

You know, Dizzy, people always say you and me are about as alike as two tadpoles, but you're in the majors and I'm bouncing around the peanut circuit.

DIZZY: Yeah, I'm going back to the St. Louis Cardinals and Broadway and you're going back to the Pittsburgh Crawfords and the chitlin' circuit—ain't no way that makes sense to me. You're a better pitcher than I ever hope to be.

SATCHEL: Why, Dizzy, my pitching philosophy is simple—keep the ball away from the bat.

DIZZY: You know, if you and I were pitching on the same team, we would cinch the pennant by July fourth and go fishing until World Series time.

SATCHEL: If you and I were on the same team, the moon would've turned to green cheese and we'd be eating it. Let's go play ball!

After the demonstration, we discuss the process of developing the fictional dialogue, combining actual quotes from these men with historical information about the times and reports about their personalities.

Students then are partnered, drawing one name from each column to create a Black-and-White pair of players. They are directed to develop a hypothetical dialogue between the two players, to include the following information about each man:

- Compare and contrast the players' lives on the road:
- Travel
- Overnight lodging
- Meals
- Treatment by the locals
- What team did he play for during the regular season? What position?
- What skills or abilities would have/should have these men respected in each other?

The dialogues are open-ended, and students may decide when/where the conversation would theoretically take place: before or after the game, during warm-ups, etc.

During the first session, each student researches one man, finding the answers to these questions and any other facts that can make the dialogue more interesting. During the following session, the partners work together to craft the dialogue and fill in needed information. My job is to circulate constantly, answering questions, posing questions of my own, and helping to locate needed material.

Of course my instructions always include the "make sure your language is appropriate to school" speech, and I continue to enforce that as I patrol and coach. The quotes from the players that are supplied within the research material will help to define and shape the language and attitudes of the players.

As the dialogues near completion, rehearsals begin. Each man's personality and attitude should be represented as accurately as possible, making him come alive for the audience. We investigate voice inflections and postures that will help portray the players (see "The Art of Expressions and Emotions in Storytelling" by Diane Williams in *The Storytelling Classroom: Applications across the Curriculum* [Libraries Unlimited, 2006] for ideas on how to do this).

Finally, the dialogues are performed! Since memorization is not required, the students can concentrate on delivering their lines with expression and meaning. I always require that the audience (including the classroom teacher and me) provide positive feedback. Questions can follow if desired, allowing the presenters to delve more deeply into the experiences of their subjects.

History is about listening to and connecting with the voices of humanity; researching, creating, and bringing those voices to life can make it meaningful and relevant to students. Making history personal by stepping into another person's shoes and speaking his words encourages empathy as students come face to face with the inequities of the Jim Crow era. Hopefully, they also become more aware of and sensitive to modern social injustice when they encounter it.

ASSESSMENT

The process is as important as the product. Observe the way in which the pairs work together, struggle with disagreements, reach compromises, or persuade each other to accept differing points of view. Assessment can be based on the core components of cooperative learning:

- positive interdependence
- group processing
- appropriate use of social skills
- face-to-face interaction
- individual and group accountability

The dialogue can be evaluated with a rubric that includes the criteria required in the lesson (above); the public speaking rubric would include

- Student speaks loudly and clearly so that everyone can hear.
- Student speaks fluently and expressively.
- Student "creates" the character through vocal and physical expression.
- Student makes eye contact with the audience.
- Student seems comfortable and relaxed in front of the listeners
- Student keeps listeners' attention throughout.

The real product is a deeper appreciation of the need for social justice and equality. Overhearing a student say, "That wasn't fair!" while researching the lives of the Negro League players is proof enough for me that the lesson is being learned.

RESOURCES

All of Bobby's print resources above, plus...

Kelley, Brent. *Voices from the Negro Leagues: Conversations with 52 Baseball Standouts of the Period 1924-1960.* Jefferson, NC: MacFarland, 2005.

Kelley, Brent. *The Negro Leagues Revisited: Conversations with 66 More Baseball Standouts of the Period 1924-1960.* Jefferson, NC: MacFarland, 2010.

Baseball Almanac: Baseball Quotes http://www.baseball-almanac.com/quomenu.shtml

Norfolk, Sherry, Diane Williams, Jane Stenson. *The Storytelling Classroom: Applications across the Curriculum.*Englewood, CO: Libraries Unlimited, 2006.

Baseball-Reference.com http://www.baseball-reference.com

Negro League Baseball Players Association www.nlbpa.com

NLBDotCom www.negroleaguebaseball.com

***SHERRY NORFOLK** is coauthor and coeditor of this book! Read her bio at the end of the book and find out more at www.sherrynorfolk.com.*

Expectation and Surprise

Andy Offutt Irwin

with Lisa Johnson, Monique Hodge, Ingrid Nixon, Margo Olmsted, Marjorie Shaefer

"We've spent a generation trying to reorganize schools to make them better, but the truth is people learn from the people they love."

DAVID BROOKS, SOCIAL ANIMAL

Now, isolating quotes is dangerous business. I was working on this piece when I read the sentence above in an excerpt from the book in the New Yorker. The book isn't about education per se, rather, it's about socialization. But that sentence jumped out at me as a former child who struggled in school, and who is now the father of a fifth grade boy who is sensitive to how people – especially his teachers—feel about him. So, on impulse, I stuck it on my Facebook status. Holy mother of Maria Montessori! There was a rash of rash opinions (Facebook lends itself to that). Some of these opinions were sent to me as messages, some put up on my wall. I was taken aback when it bothered so many people. But, alas, there is a whole lot of polarization out there, and so many chips are upon so many shoulders; everything is laced in politics.

But there is a reason this sentence struck me.

I will only say that the incident I am about to describe occurred in the early 2010s in the spring of the year. In describing all of this, I will change the name of the city and state (and I have made sure I have deleted the gig from my website calendar). I will say that it took place in a first grade classroom of a Title I school. I will also say that the teacher was white; most of the students were not. The teacher was also a veteran with over twenty years of experience and was, at that time, the school's Teacher of the Year.

I was there for a weeklong literacy residency in which I help the children write their own songs, working for one hour in each of five first-grade classrooms. I was to do a program I made up called, "I Got Those Low Down Dirty Emergent Reader Blues." This had been developed in a Title I school in some eight years before. This was not my first rodeo.

When I begin this program, it behooves me to teach a teeny bit of American pop-musicology. On the chalkboard (or dry-erase board, or SMART Board[1]) I draw a quick outline of the continental United States. On that I draw the Mississippi River in order to demonstrate how the music we think of as uniquely American was carried up north on barges and boats. If I can, I always draw the river with blue chalk and I put white sparkles in the Delta, so it can shine like a National Guitar.[2]

Now, it is not a perfect map of the U.S., so I always tell the children, "This is not to scale," but I believe my U.S. is passable enough. It is certainly recognizable. Think: a caricature of the United States. When drawing it, one must always remember to make a southerly dip on the right side of the northern border for the Great Lakes, and it is most important not to make your Florida bigger than your Texas. Gentle Reader, I have just now taken a break from writing to draw a rendition of said map, and not to toot my own horn, but my U.S. outline is equally as good, if not better, than some I have seen rendered by real-live day-job artists and graphic designers. I mean mine is easily as good as the map Natasha Fatale and Boris Badenov used when pursuing Rocky and Bullwinkle across the country.[3] And I feel quite confident that it is superior to the 48-contiguous-state-shaped white portion in the center of the Kroger gas station logo, which my eleven year-old son has keenly observed, looks like a diaper.

Did I say it was a spring day?... Yes, yes I did. It may have been late in the spring as I recall. Everyone who has ever worked in lower elementary grades can tell you, there is a big difference in the skill levels of a late spring class, than a September or October class. Even if you're not in the education biz, this should seem obvious. These children should almost be ready for the second grade.

So I drew my map on the board, turned around, and asked, "What is that?"

Silence.

"C'mon, y'all."

One kid. "A map?"

"Right, a map. A map of what?"

Again, no one answered.

I looked at the teacher whose eyes moved across the classroom back to me. Her mouth went lipless and flat, and she shook her head slowly, in a dismissive and patronizing float. She seemed to be saying, "These poor underprivileged children."

I felt my heart race and my face flush. Yes, in making my way to the school, I had driven through the children's neighborhood—the public housing projects. I could tell these kids were underprivileged. Under the gun. Underdogs. And without the School Breakfast and Lunch Program, I could guess many were underfed during weekends and the summer. And now, with their very own teacher's low expectations for their ability to learn, I knew, in this classroom, they were underserved.

So, for the next ten minutes my lesson plan changed. Really, it took ten minutes, tops.

I said, "This is most of the United States of America." Then I drew and explained Hawaii and Alaska.

I drew their very own state. I had them name it. Then I drew their county and finally their town. We named them all in unison in rapid succession. Then a silly game ensued, almost like Simon Says.

I would say, "Country!"

They would say, "The United States of America!"

"State!"

"New Hampshire!"[4]

"City!"

"Grover's Corners!"

"County!"

"Wilder County!"

After this game, these children knew their city, their county, their state, and their country. The next day, I brought in my road atlas from the car. The kids all huddled around. I knew they would remember this forever.

Now, I am not a teacher. I'm just a goofy showman with a guitar, a squeaky hammer, and an apple puppet who gets to go into schools a few times a year to do the same five or six different programs. It is easy for me to be liked by the students. But for those in-the-trenches educators, the successful, liked teachers—these are the ones who expect a lot from their students. And the children, even before they can express this with language, like these teachers because they know that they are respected. And the children know they are respected because the teachers challenge them and expect the best from them.

And after visiting that school, where I went from being a songster to a lame cartographer, it occurred to me that a story I have been telling for years is really a story about expectations. That story is called "How Marguerite Became a Recovering Racist at Dr. Terror's House."

* * *

I am a white guy from a small town in Georgia who was born in 1957. As a low-achieving elementary student, I was at the right time and the right place to have a certain perspective on school integration (or "desegregation," as some people chose to call it in order put a different spin on it). I put the character of myself in the story from this perspective. In the story, I incorporate real social events and school practices of the time. Tracking in elementary schools was prominent in the South during Integration, and it quickly became a means of segregating students within a school. There were five tracked groups when I was in the fifth grade, Group 5 being the highest achievers. That year, I was in Group 2. There were six groups when I was in the sixth grade. Because integration instantly tracked the black kids into the lower groups[5], I had been pushed up to Group 4. Shortly after that sixth-grade year began, Cynthia Banks joined us in Group 4. She was the first African American in our school to have been placed higher than Group 3. But this did not happen without a good deal of wheel-squeaking by her parents.

So, in the story, as in real life, I was a drummer in the band. And in real life I became good friends with Johnny Norrington, a black kid from the black school. Johnny had a brother named Kenny. If you must know, the situations are real, as well as my friendship with Johnny and Kenny, but this is where fact pretty much stops.

Marguerite Van Camp is my fictional aunt. When I tell stories about her in a present-time setting, she is an eighty-five year old widow, and has just graduated from medical school along with a few of her fellow widows. She and her girlfriends have opened their own hospital called Southern White Old Lady Hospital.[6] But in this story that takes place during my childhood, she is around forty-five.

Let me tell you, that handy-dandy fictional character is a powerful device. In stories in which I am trying to make a point (and I certainly want to avoid being "preachy"), the character of Marguerite serves to move anecdotes and action away from the character of me; that keeps me from ever being a self-aggrandizing hero. The other practical use of having fictional characters doing my dirty work is it keeps me innocent, especially if I have something to say that may make anybody in my audience uncomfortable. The audience's willing suspension of disbelief means that Marguerite can say just about anything. She is just such a sweet, genteel lady, and, of course, well, she means well.

Here's an example that I use in the story. In real life, when I was twelve, my older cousin, Sid, and his wife, Debbie, flew me out to Denver to stay with them for a month. It was my first time out of the South, and my accent was pretty thick. One of the moms of a neighbor-kid I was playing with there sneered at me and asked me where I was from. When I told her Georgia, her retort was, "Everybody in Georgia is a bigot."

I didn't have the language, the maturity (or the talk-backitude) to tell her how prejudiced, and flat-out mean that was. And yes, the best come-backs always come to one way too late. So, in the story, I fictionalize that event by having Marguerite and her best lady-friends go on a trip to New York to celebrate the year they all turn forty. In the story, the ladies are standing in the box office line for *Man of La Mancha*. The woman behind the glass asks Marguerite where she is from. When Marguerite answers her, the box office woman gives that same retort: "Everybody in Georgia is a bigot."

Marguerite in turn says, "Oh. You mean just the white people, or everybody?"

Marguerite ponders that and begins her journey on the road to becoming a recovering racist.

In the 1950s and '60s, there was a whole kids' movie matinee circuit with—not just movies—but live horror shows. One of the purveyors of these kids' horror shows was a man from Charlotte, NC named Philip Morris, who had a show called, "That Crazy Mixed-up Dr. Evil and His Terrors of the Unknown." (In the story, I changed his name to "Dr. Terror.")[7] Responsible parents would never let their kids go to such a thing. My mom was fine with it.

The movie house of my childhood, where I whiled away many a Saturday afternoon, was segregated; the black kids sat in the balcony while the white kids were downstairs. Then, as now, whenever one group of children is physically above another group of children, gravity occurs. This fact was the catalyst for the story. And, truth be told, I didn't start out with any idea of making up something to bring any social injustice to light (although our values come through in what we write, don't they?) Rather, I simply thought the idea of talking about Dr. Evil and gravity and snakes could be funny.

So I started to think about it.

So here's my evil thought process for building the story.

- Have Dr. Terror throw rubber snakes from the stage into the audience.[8]
- Remembering the situation of the balcony, and, again, taking advantage of the fact of gravity, have Johnny and Kenny in the balcony dropping real snakes on the white children.
- Create a situation in which Marguerite comes into the movie theatre at just the right time to discover the real snakes, and learn that Johnny and Kenny are responsible for them. Marguerite, being who she us, is impressed by the resourcefulness of Johnny and Kenny.

They have acted beyond her expectations.

Children's author Rick Walton, in his essay titled simply, "What is Humor?" says, "Humor is surprise without threat or promise."

We storytellers who think of ourselves as humorists[9] go beyond simple comedy when the surprise elements of our stories help listeners change their expectations.

INSTRUCTIONAL PLAN

Lisa Johnson, Monique Hodge, Ingrid Nixon, Margo Olmsted, Marjorie Shaefer

OBJECTIVES *for Middle School and High School*

Students will

- reflect on their own behavior, thinking about what influences the way they perceive others, and about how these perceptions impact their interactions and relationships.
- explore the influence of people and environment on their personal development, making an effort to understand others and their beliefs, feelings, and convictions.

MATERIALS

- photos of kids around the same age as the students in your class. The set of photos should represent a wide range of ethnicities, income levels, etc. A good website for a wide variety of free photo downloads is iStockphoto® at www.istockphoto.com—keyword: teenagers only

We all make judgments all of the time—it's the human condition. We look at other people and create instant expectations about who they are, what they are, and how they behave based on the color of their skin, the clothes they wear, the way they walk or stand. This is an efficiency mechanism—we simply don't have time to collect all of the data. But many of these judgments are based on faulty, often unconscious, preconceptions that get in the way of really getting to know one another.

This activity is designed to help students become conscious of the judgments they make, and the ways these affect their interactions with others.

Distribute a photo to each student, with instructions to write a first-person story about the pictured person: "Writing as that person, discuss your family life, interests, personality, hopes, dreams, and expectations. What assumptions do people make about you? Are these assumptions true? What do you think about yourself? Do you live up to (or down to) the expectations of others?"

Once the stories are written, pair up the students and ask them to read their stories to each other.

Discussion:

- How did it feel to be in that person's shoes? Why did you make these judgments about your character?
- Then, the pairs will collaborate to create a story about what happens when their two characters meet—in the cafeteria, at a football game, in the mall. How will these characters respond to each other and why?
- Share these stories with the class.

Discussion:

- What false assumptions were made? How could these be harmful? How can we avoid making and acting on these assumptions? How do we get past our preconceptions? Are there any circumstances under which a bias is acceptable?

ASSESSMENT

- Ask students to journal about this experience. Have they discovered any biases within themselves, and if so, do they want to /need to change them? What steps can they take to change their attitudes?
- Ask each student to write on a slip of paper what he/she intends to change and how. These are sealed in individual envelopes and collected by the teacher to be opened by the individual students 3-6 months later. Follow-up journaling and discussion will help students assess their progress and determine next steps.

RESOURCES

iStockphoto® at www.istockphoto.com

"What is humor?" http://www.rickwalton.com/lang/whathumo.htm

1 As with *PowerPoint*, There is a bit of a learning curve with *SMART Boards*. Here's something you never hear people say when they use a chalkboard: "Whoa, we're having technical difficulties. Heh. Heh...um ... bear with me. Sorry..."

2 Thank you, Paul Simon.

3 All roads lead to Frostbite Falls, MN.

4 Remember, I have changed the actual place. Pay attention.

5 This tracking occurred after very short "interviews" with the black students after they were transferred to the new all-white school.

6 In the thinking and writing of white people, *white* is the default, and that is the problem. Also, while I'm at it, one would think, with these over-the-top details, folks would know that Marguerite is a fictional character, but you'd be surprised, unless, of course, you are one of those folks. In that case, I'm sorry.

7 When I wrote the story *Mike Myers* had a character named *Dr. Evil* from his Austin Powers series of movies, so I changed my character's name. In hindsight, it was a bad call. Regret is bitter.

8 The real Dr. Evil of my childhood threw snakes—something that would no longer happen in our litigious culture (*sigh*).

9 The difference between a *humorist* and a *comedian*: the humorist performs in more public libraries, and there isn't a three-drink minimum.

***ANDY OFFUTT IRWIN** is an award-winning storyteller, musician, record producer, and show-off from Covington, Georgia. Among other gigs, he has done several stints as a Featured Teller at the National Storytelling Festival; a Guest Artist at La Guardia High School for Art, Music and Performing Arts in New York (The "FAME!" School); and a Keynote Speaker/Performer at the Library of Congress-Viburnum Foundation Conference on Family Literacy. His old straight jobs include: Artist-In-Residence in Theatre at Oxford College of Emory University (1991—2007), and writer, director, performer for SAK Theatre at Walt Disney World (1984-1989). He thinks he's funny.*

***LISA JOHNSON, MONIQUE HODGE, INGRID NIXON, MARGO OLMSTED, MARJORIE SHAEFER** were members of a graduate course on storytelling in the classroom at East Tennessee State University. They collaboratively developed this lesson plan in response to Andy's performance as Teller in Residence at the International Storytelling Center.*

The Queen Bee

A GRIMM'S TALE

or

Starting the Year Off Right in Kindergarten

Jane Stenson

OBJECTIVES

Students will

- help young children regard their classmates as friends with whom they will spend the year.
- help egocentric children develop a sense of themselves as cooperative, caring members of a group.
- develop listening skills.
- understand and follow the teacher's expectations about behavior.
- imbed social studies goals into our daily school lives.

MATERIALS

- Burningham, John. *Mr. Gumpy's Outing.* New York: Henry Holt and Company, 1970.
- tagboard, construction paper, markers and glue for the storyboard

INSTRUCTIONAL PLAN

At the beginning of the school year (in fact, the second day of school) I, the teacher, tell the story "The Queen Bee" to my kindergarten class because I want to give children the opportunity to be their best selves; I want to tell them that this is the behavior I expect in school. I want to give us (children and teacher) a shared experience and shared language to talk about how we treat each other; so, telling "The Queen Bee" is my first step in teaching proactive conflict resolution procedures. I also want to begin teaching narrative structure and this story's structure is abundantly clear. It also contains vocabulary that five and six year olds will have to determine through context.

The hero who is the third son is filled with compassion for living things—his father, his brothers, the creatures of the earth, sea and air, and the people he meets. It is his compassion or caring that guides him to be fair and honest, to be responsible and to act as a good citizen in the enchanted place he and his brothers enter. He cares and therefore acts so deeply that the land "where there was nothing that was not stone" is restored or transformed by his actions to life in the fields and the manor house and in relationships.

The Queen Bee

retold by Jane Stenson

Once upon a time there lived a man with three sons. The two eldest were spendthrifts and n'er-do-wells. They frittered away their time and squandered their money. The youngest son was hardworking and cheerful.

One day the two older boys went to their father and said, "We are going out into the world to seek our fortune." Their father wished them well and off they went. The father was happy to be with his youngest son because they accomplished much and were pleased with each other. But after a time, the son said to his father that he too wished to go out into the world, find his brothers, and seek his fortune. The father didn't want him to go, but he gave his son his blessing, wished him well, and off the lad went.

Soon he met up with his brothers who said, "What are you doing here?" The youngest brother replied that he wanted to join them and make his way in the world and seek his fortune. The older brothers laughed and laughed and said, "We who are older haven't found our fortune yet, what makes you think you can find yours?"

"Nevertheless,' said the youngest, "I would like to try." So they all walked on together.

They came to an anthill. All the ants were busy working. "Say," said the oldest brother, "Let's scruff up these anthills and kill all the ants!"

"No," said the youngest, "The ants have done us no harm. We must leave them alone."

"Oh no, you're no fun," said the eldest brother.

The three walked on and soon came to a lake where many ducks were swimming. "Oooo, look at that!" said the older boys, "We're really hungry. Let's shoot some of those ducks and roast them for our dinner."

"No!" said the youngest, "They have done us no harm. We must leave them alone."

"Here we go again," said the older boys.

They continued walking and espied a tree with honey oozing down the side and a large beehive in its boughs. "Ah!" said the older brothers. "Let's build a fire at the base of the tree and smoke out those bees."

"No!" said the youngest brother, "The bees have done us no harm. Leave them alone."

"That's enough!" said the older brothers. They were disgusted. "You better decide if you're coming with us or if you should go home. You are no fun at all."

On the three of them walked and after a while they came to a large manor house surrounded by fields, which was completely made out of stone. Everything on the outside was made of stone: the grass, the trees, the fields, the sheep, the cows. There was nothing that was not stone.

The brothers walked to the front door and knocked. When no one answered they opened the door and went in. Everything on the inside was made of stone: the drapes, the tables, the chairs, the light fixtures, the rug, even the cookies on the plate. There was nothing that was not stone.

They walked through every part of the manor house until they came to a closed wooden door at the back of the house. They knocked lightly and opened the door. Inside the room was an old man seated at a table who asked what they wanted.

The brothers said, "We have come to seek our fortune."

"Well," said the old man, "You may have come to the right place. You see, I used to be a king. Many years ago a spell was placed on this castle. Everything was turned to stone except for me and my three daughters. If you can accomplish three tasks between sunup and sundown, you can break

continued

the magic spell. If you succeed, you will inherit half of my property and may marry one of my daughters. However, if you fail any task, you too will be turned to stone."

"Oh I would surely like to try!" said the eldest brother.

The next morning at sunup the oldest brother was given the first task: to find one thousand pearls that had been scattered about the castle grounds. The brother searched all day, and by sundown he had found only two hundred pearls. He was instantly turned to stone.

On the next day the middle brother searched and he found only five hundred pearls. He was turned to stone.

On the third morning the youngest brother went to the front steps of the manor house and sat on the steps. He put his head in his hands and a tear slid down his cheek. The queen of the ants went to him and asked him why he was crying.

"Because I have to find 1000 pearls by sundown or I will be turned to stone. My older brothers tried and failed and I don't see how I can accomplish the task. I don't think I can break the spell."

The queen of the ants said, "You saved our lives and now, we'll save yours." All the ants went throughout the grounds gathering pearls and gave them to the youngest brother who gave them to the old man.

The next morning the old man met the boy on the bank of the lake. "My king's ring was thrown out into the lake by the enchantress and you must find it by sundown or you will be turned to stone." The boy did not know what to do.

Just then, the king of the ducks saw his difficulty and swam to him. The king of the ducks said, "You saved our lives and now we'll save yours." The ducks dove to the bottom of the lake and dove to the bottom of the lake. It took all day. Just as the sun was beginning to set, a duck rose to the surface with the ring in its beak and gave it to the youngest son who gave it to the king who put it on his finger.

On the third day the youngest son entered the king's room for the third and final task. "Stop there at the door," said the king who was seated with his three daughters who looked exactly alike. "On the lips of one of my daughters is a drop of syrup. On the lips of another is a drop of sugar water. And, the other has a drop of honey on her lips. Stand in the doorway and choose which princess has a drop of honey on her lips. Remember, if you accomplish this task, you will inherit half of my kingdom and may marry one of my daughters. If you fail you will be turned into stone."

The young man had no idea which princess had honey on her lips, but just then through an open window flew the queen bee. She flew straight to the daughter with the honey and alighted on her lip. The youngest son identified her and the spell was broken!

Everything was returned to its natural form: the sheep, the grass, the trees, the chairs and tables, even the cookies on the plate. His brothers came alive. In due course the youngest brother married the princess with the sweet honey on her lips and they all lived happily ever after.

INSTRUCTIONAL PLAN

Week One

FIRST DAY OF SCHOOL: This little poem hangs on chart paper behind the teacher's chair for all to see/read it:

Hurt No Living Thing
Christina Rosetti

Hurt no living thing:
Labybird, nor butterfly,
Nor moth with dusty wing.
No cricket chirping cheerily,
Nor grasshopper so light of leap,
No dancing gnats, Nor beetles fat,
Nor harmless worms that creep.

SECOND DAY OF SCHOOL: Tell the folktale "The Queen Bee."

THIRD DAY OF SCHOOL: My intern and I get inside the puppet theatre (an old-style, emptied TV console) (very funny for the children to have the teachers on their knees doing a puppet show) with paper puppets taped on craft sticks and tell the story on our knees while the children watch the puppet show as if they were watching TV. I know by now that they know the story and can tell it. In fact, when we say the words a bit differently, some children correct us! I want that flexibility to be part of our lives together as well.

FOURTH DAY OF SCHOOL: Discuss the story: what did you like? What happened? Do you think there was a real place where there was nothing that was not stone? What is the story about? I accept every answer.

FIFTH DAY OF SCHOOL: Choose six children to create a kindergarten-style storyboard. Using the plot and a six-frame basic storyboard format have each child draw a picture and dictate the language to 'tell' the story on an 8" X 12" piece of colored paper. When completed, I cut it out in an irregular shape, glue their pictures/words to a big (24" X 36") piece of tagboard. At the "rug" time later in the morning, the children will then 'tell' the story to their classmates…to much applause! "What great storytellers!"

Six-framed Kindergarten storyboard

Sometimes more than six children want to participate!

One of the picture books I read this week is *Mr. Gumpy's Outing* by John Burningham. It's about Mr. Gumpy taking many animals on a boat ride. As each asks and receives permission to get on the boat, Mr. Gumpy cautions the sheep "Yes you may come, but no bleating," or to the goat "Yes, you may come but no kicking," and so on with each animal. Everything proceeds smoothly for a while, but then the sheep bleats and the goat kicks, etc, until the boat tips and everyone falls in the water. Mr. Gumpy says, "Well, let's dry off; come with me and let's have some tea."

Week Two

On the playground and in the classroom by now someone has pushed or kicked or taken a block or knocked someone's work. It's important to tell children that these conflicts are a natural part of being together in a community. Some children are certain the other child "did it on purpose." Here is the opportunity to use the language of the story: "Oh, don't shoot (kick or push) him, he has done us no harm," referencing "The Queen Bee."

Conflict resolution procedures are best learned in the moment with a follow-up with the entire class. First, assuming there's no physical injury, bring the two children together calmly. One child states the offense from her point of view. The second child states the offense from his point of view. Each must listen to the other and each must look at the other. Then I ask them how to solve the problem. If they are silent, I say "Together, you created the situation, and together you two brave children can figure out the solution." I wait. Because the children want to get on with their play, they often smile at each other, offer a quick apology, and run away. But, if they need help with the language of processing the situation or if it's emotionally hard to say, "I don't like it when you..." I will help them with their language. However, I will not take over the negotiation because I believe they can solve their own problems. "You created this situation together and you can solve it together."

School is a public place and being in a group, albeit a large group, means that very little is private. So, back on the rug with all the children, I often, but not always, ask the two perpetrators to tell the class what happened and how they solved the problem. My role as teacher is to care about the children and the transaction; I accept both children and keep this conversation serious but light...because conflicts happen; they are a natural part of being together. Yes, I repeated that statement! The children need to recognize that solutions happen too, and that they can be part of the solution. This is how I build the community, two children at a time, bringing their dilemma to the entire class. The children need to understand that their concerns will be addressed at school with the teacher and with each other.

Cooperation (or how to solve problems with imagination so that every person involved can succeed and/or get his needs satisfied): Here is a math activity that helps me assess the children's counting ability as well as their styles of cooperation. It's from *Creating the Peaceable School* by Richard Bodine, Donna Crawford and Fred Schrumpf. I hang a big piece of paper and print the word COOPERATION in the center and ask children what the word means, and to share an example of when they were cooperating with another person to accomplish a task.

Next, I divide children in groups of three children each. Their task is to face each other and clench their fist. They shake their fist up and down counting "One, Two, Three, Four" On the count of four each puts out any number of fingers from zero to five. Their goal is to get 11 fingers out. Each group keeps trying until they get 11, and they may only count, and not talk, during the math play. [At a higher math level, have each group try to total 23 fingers, with each person using both hands.]

After most groups are successful, we talk about "What made the activity difficult?" And "What helped your group succeed?" I tell them that cooperation or working together as well as accurate counting are very important.

ASSESSMENT

I return the children to "The Queen Bee" and ask them to think about cooperation, and why the animals of the land, the water and the sky cooperated with the third son. The children's answers tell me what they have understood in the story and how they can apply it in their lives. Assessment is tricky in this regard; if a conflict happens and the children are not sophisticated in their handling of it, I re-teach the procedure, and I share our common language about "Hurt no living thing" or "They have done us no harm. Leave them alone." Learning to handle conflicts and how to speak up to mediate and solve problems is a life-long quest. It needs to begin when children are young and hope is high.

RESOURCES

Bodine, Richard, Crawford, Donna K, and Schrumpf, Fred. *Creating the Peaceable School: A Comprehensive Program for Teaching Conflict Resolution.* Champaigne, IL: Research Press, 1994.

Burmingham, John. *Mr. Gumpy's Outing.* New York: Henry Holt and Company, 1970.

Jane Stenson is coauthor, coeditor of this book and a former kindergarten teacher! Read bio at the end of the book. www.janestenson.com

What's Normal?

Donna Washington

I was cleaning my kitchen one spring day shortly after my family moved to Durham, North Carolina. The little blonde girl from across the fence, who was four at the time, came over to play with my son. After a while, they were sitting at the kitchen table having a snack. My son left to build with his Legos and the little girl turned to me.

"Miss Donna?"

"Yes?"

"How come you are brown and Devin's father isn't?"

I smiled. "Well, I'm brown because my parents are brown. Devin's father isn't brown because his parents aren't brown." She considered that for a moment and then looked confused. I waited for her to ask a follow-up question.

"You're not the same color," she informed me.

"I know." I waited again. I had no idea if she was having a problem or if she was just curious. It turned out that she was curious. Perhaps she wasn't aware that I knew we were two different colors. Perhaps she just wanted to make sure that I was seeing what she was seeing. Either way, she seemed satisfied and hasn't brought it up again in the last twelve years.

This little girl was trying to adjust to a reality she'd either never seen or never noticed. To her eyes it seemed abnormal. She wasn't sure what to make of it. In her home, everyone was the same color. Why was it different at my house? She is hardly alone in this. Many people assume that what happens in their home or community is normal.

Does your family go to church on Sunday? Does anyone in your family like to watch football or NASCAR, or baseball or hockey? Boys eat lots of food, and like sports, right? Girls are concerned about their hair and like shopping for clothes or buying shoes, right? Are the things I just listed normal to you?

Do the people in your home go to worship on Saturday? Do you use prayer shawls or have shrines in your home? Are the girls allowed to wear pants? Do the boys always keep their heads covered? Are the members of your family different colors? Are there two moms or two dads in your home? Do your grandparents live with you? Do the kids look completely different from the parents? What if your family doesn't own a television? What if they live in a mobile home? What if the kids don't go to school outside of the house? Are the things I just listed normal to you?

The longer we live near each other, the more normal 'different' becomes. The only thing some people find more frightening than 'different' is the idea that things they think are 'different' will become normal. It is easier to be afraid of different and to try to destroy it or stop it than to find out about it and understand it.

Those who fear that different will become normal have a reason to fear. Each generation of Americans has become more and more accepting of the fact that our country is full of people from different places. We find them interesting. We learn about them and we accept them. When they are no longer 'different,' we even join them, or ask them to join us. Together, we keep creating America. We build bridges across cultures and traditions. We build understanding across religions and we create Americans who are caught between traditions, religions and sometimes communities. We create Americans who are different.

There was a time when being biracial in America was considered a shameful thing. There was a time when it was illegal for people from two different races to marry. There was a time when it was believed that if you were biracial, you would not amount to anything. Being a biracial person was not considered 'normal.' Well, in 2008, Americans elected a biracial president.

When President Barack Hussein Obama was running for his office, his opponents said many things about him. They gave as many reasons as they could find to suggest that voting for him was a bad idea. Nobody suggested that voters should not choose him because he was biracial. Biracial Americans are becoming a more common occurrence all over America. There is no doubt that our future is one of people blurring the lines between races, religions and traditions. In many places in America, that is already normal.

For some people, different will always be scary. Others will demonize it. Some people hide from the thing that is different. Then there are the people who cause the most trouble. They claim to *know* why different is dangerous. They stare at the different through their small window of fear and believe that what they see is the truth. They are like the five people in this story from India:

Once, there were five learned blind men. They wanted to know what an elephant was like.

One of them touched the trunk and said, "An elephant is flexible and shaped like a snake."

One touched the tail and said, "An elephant is skinny and hard like a stick."

One touched the leg and said, "An elephant is like the trunk of a tree."

One touched the side and said, "An elephant is large and flat like a wall."

One man touched the tusk and said, "An elephant is hard and sharp like a tool."

Each walked away, convinced he understood the elephant.

That's where the story usually ends, but I've always believed there should be one more part. What happened when the five men sat down to discuss the elephant? Did they fight? Did they argue? Did they laugh? Did they call each other fools? Did each one decide that if their companions didn't agree with their point of view they were evil? Did they work together to draw a picture of the elephant? What did they do?

America is a big country. We have so many different traditions it is impossible to know all of them. We eat different kinds of food, live in different houses, love in different kinds of families and practice different traditions. Often, we see our small part of America and think it is the only true normal. We are convinced our small community is the whole elephant. The truth is, the only thing that is normal in America is that we are all different.

***DONNA L. WASHINGTON** is a published author, artist teacher and professional storyteller who started her career in 1989 after graduating from Northwestern University. She has performed and taught all over the world. Donna also has seven multiple-award winning CDs. Her publishing credits include: **The Story of Kwanzaa, A Pride of African Tales** and **Li'l Rabbit's Kwanzaa** published by HarperCollins Children's Books, and **A Big Spooky House** published by Hyperion Books for Children. She lives in Durham, North Carolina with her husband and manager David, their children Devin and Darith, and their two mischievous cats Love Bug and Flash. www.DLstoryteller.com.*

About the Authors

JANE STENSON and **SHERRY NORFOLK** are considered two of the preeminent experts on the applications of storytelling in the classroom. Along with Diane Williams, they co-authored the award-winning *Storytelling Classroom: Applications Across the Curriculum* (Libraries Unlimited, 2006) and *Literacy Development in the Storytelling Classroom* (Libraries Unlimited, 2009). And, here they go again, this time taking a hard look at the intersection of storytelling and social studies.

JANE STENSON is the storyteller at Baker Demonstration School in Wilmette, Il. Storytelling (Jane's, the faculty's and the children's) is a major dimension of the school curriculum. Every day she tries to find just the right story to match children's interests and behavior! Teachers sign up; she goes to classrooms and tells stories. Jane presents storytelling programs associated with curricular goals for Pre-Kindergarten through Eighth Grade, such as Immigration, Ancient Greece, Rocks & Minerals. Further, she collaborates with teachers on storytelling projects such as the Fourth Grade study of the Solar System where she helped students enjoy and learn constellation myths. As producer of a school and community Storytelling Series, Jane brings touring storytellers into the school for mini-residencies and concerts. Every day she does the work necessary to encourage teachers and storytellers to work together and share knowledge about how children learn best: *through storytelling.*

As a long time educator—a practitioner—Jane has taught high school English and history, Early Childhood classes, including kindergarten from 1995–2010, and, at National-Louis University with which the Baker school is affiliated. Constantly on the lookout for new relationships between storytelling and education, Jane understands well that children learn best through a story, the frame for all content and social learning. Jane currently serves as NSN's YES! SIG co-chair, that's Youth, Educators', and Storytellers' Alliance. www.janestenson.com or email stenson.stories@gmail.com.

SHERRY NORFOLK is an internationally acclaimed storyteller, appearing at the International Storytelling Center, the Singapore Storytelling Festival, and many more festivals, schools, libraries and universities nationwide. In addition to an electric stage presence, she embodies the term "teaching artist"—that is, an artist who can not only talk the talk but walk the walk. Sherry leads residencies and workshops internationally, introducing children and adults to story making and storytelling. She is on the roster of seven state arts councils, a testimony to her value as a teaching artist. Her dedication to and deep interest in children and literacy have been recognized with national awards from the American Library Association, the Association for Library Service for Children, the National Association of Counties, and the Florida Library Association. Sherry and her husband Bobby are coauthors of *The Moral of the Story: Folktales for Character Development* (August House, 1999) and six picture books. Sherry is past Chair of the National Storytelling Network Board of Directors, and recipient of an NSN Oracle Award for Distinguished National Service. She is Adjunct Professor in the Integrated Arts in Learning program at Lesley University, and in the Storytelling program at East Tennessee State University. Visit her website at www.sherrynorfolk.com or e-mail shnorfolk@aol.com.

Index

F

G

H

I

J

K

L

M

N

O

P

R

S

T

U

V

W

Y

Z